sell BIGGER

Unlock repeat business by transforming how you communicate

sell BIGGER

Unlock repeat business by transforming how you communicate

ANGELA SUTTON, PH.D

SELL BIGGER

Published by Best Seller Publishing®, St. Augustine, FL
Best Seller Publishing® is a registered trademark.
Printed in the United States of America.
ISBN: 978-1-956649-25-3

Printed and published in the United States of America

For more information, please write:
Best Seller Publishing®
53 Marine Street
St. Augustine, FL 32084
or call 1 (626) 765-9750
Visit us online at: www.BestSellerPublishing.org

SELL BIGGER

"At the end of the day people won't remember what you said or did, they will remember how you made them feel."

— Maya Angelou

Contents

Bonus Resources

Attention, book readers!

Register to download free bonus materials here:

www.marketfastforward.com/freestuff

Bonus Materials include:

- Printable PDF copies of the Action Sheets found in this book
- Links to challenges and courses that accelerate your ability to put the "Sell Bigger" framework into action in your business
- Text copies of the examples in the book, so you can use them as a basis for your own communications

INTRODUCTION

"We feel like you take us for granted,"

... a customer who had been using our software for almost three years remarked, as we prepared to renew their software license contract.

It was not for our lack of trying to stay in touch.

We'd call ... hitting their voicemail 70% of the time. Recorded voicemails left were returned 20% of the time.

We'd send helpful emails weekly to keep them up to date on new software features.

We'd send videos every 2 weeks to show them how they could use our software to solve common problems.

Our help was apparently lost amid the crush of the customer's exploding email inbox and their full calendar.

The remark confirmed my suspicion and concern that this customer account might be at risk.

And yet, once we finally got talking, it turned out we had so much more that we could offer them.

If you are a software sales or marketing professional or a technology startup who is finding it difficult to get account visibility and communicate with impact to your customers, you are in good company.

You want to be a "good vendor" and show customers that you care...and yet struggle to keep their attention.

In the back of your mind, you know that selling to an *existing* customer is an easier road to take than closing a new customer.

According to a Bain & Company study, the cost to sell a product or a service to a new customer is 6-7 times more than the cost of retaining an existing customer.

And according to an Invesp study you have a 60% chance of selling more to an existing customer. Whereas, selling to a new prospect drops your success rate to < 20% .

Existing customers are 50% more likely than new ones to try a new product that you sell.

You certainly need to focus on new sales prospects, but you should first and foremost treasure and sell to the customers that you already have.

During each conversation with a customer comes the opportunity to serve them and sell more.

What can you do to get a conversation going with a current customer:

- To grab missed upsell opportunities (expansion)?
- To renew deals without having to cave on price or shrink the deal size (avoid contraction)?

- To avoid being caught off guard when a customer jumps ship (avoid churn)?

If you are a sales or marketing professional, this book will help you communicate in a way to make customers pay attention. It will help you to get conversations underway that gain account visibility and demonstrate to customers that you care.

This book will provide you with the clarity to communicate online proactively, day in, day out so that you can uncover new ways to help your customers and they then gladly spend more money with you.

The book will show you what to say and how to say it, using a framework that gets the customer's attention and is then so interesting that customers will actually consume and take action.

My domain of expertise is undoubtedly B2B software, and the examples within this book are from the software industry.

With that said, the framework that this book teaches has been applied by me as I helped clients from many other industries including semiconductor hardware businesses and veterinary practices. It works a charm!

The framework works for presentations, webinars, master-classes, emails, voicemails, whitepapers, articles *and even online sales funnel web pages*.

Most importantly, this book will show you the specifics of how to deepen your relationship and leave a lasting impression with your sales accounts so that they know you care.

Because according to a Rockefeller survey, 68% of customers who leave (churn), do so because they believe you don't care about them.

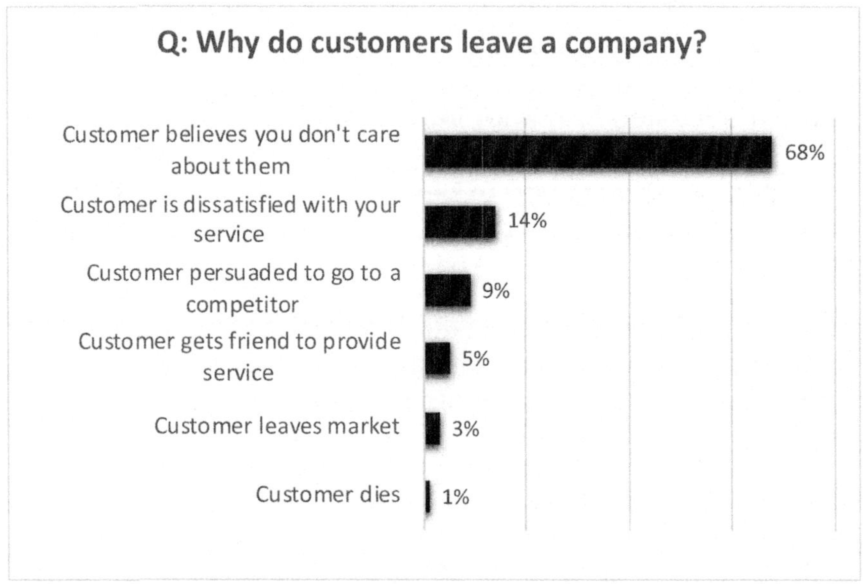

This book practices what it preaches. You won't just read and forget it.

Instead, you will put what you learn into action using the book's:

- Communication examples – email, video, voicemail, etc., that you can model to create your own
- Action sheets that let you apply what you just learned and immediately put it to work in your business

But before we get going, I want you to imagine stepping onto the stage of *Shark Tank* with your software. Right on cue, the Sharks ask about your numbers.

"How much profit do you earn on average on a single customer throughout the entire time that they are your customer?" (Your Average Customer Lifetime Value or **CLV**) and

"How much does it cost you on average to get a new customer

(Your Average Customer Acquisition Cost, or "**CAC**")?"

Why would the *Shark Tank* investors care, and why should you and your company care also about these two numbers?

Because they immediately tell you whether your company is poised to scale its revenue growth.

In general, you have a subscription software business that's ready to grow when:

> 3 x CAC < CLV
>
> where
>
> CLV = Average Customer Lifetime Value
>
> CAC = Average Customer Acquisition Cost

Indeed,
A 3:1 CLV:CAC ratio indicates a likely break-even subscription business.
A 5:1 CLV:CAC ratio, for example indicates a healthy, profitable subscription business, poised to be able to invest in scaling

A startup or brand-new product will struggle to sell against an "industry gorilla" that has brand name recognition and a huge marketing budget.

This means that its customer acquisition costs can be high.

But they don't have to be.

How did startup Apple out-market Gorilla IBM, and be perceived as a "Category King" in the personal computer space? How did they succeed while using a fraction of IBM's marketing budget?

The answer lies in how Apple *celebrated the person* that the customer strives to be, *not the product.*

Their “Apple Mac Guy vs. the PC Guy” ad series for example.

This is something that they and other successful companies such as Nike continue to do to this day.

If you are a professional starting a new venture that needs funding – or are selling to an audience where you compete with “Industry Gorilla” brands, this book will help you.

It will show you how to connect *emotionally* with your customer’s identity; to build their vision of what it will mean to them personally and professionally when they experience your product.

It will let you do this even if you have a tiny marketing budget.

It will show you how to remove sales objections, doubts, and excuses not to buy, before they can be raised, and then continue to succeed at this for as long as individuals are your customers, to increase customer lifetime value by keeping the customer around and selling them additional products.

Specifically, this book will let you:

- Master the five essential components of every communication so that you use these like clockwork to get your customers’ attention, keep it, and drive to the next step in your sales funnel, rather than overwhelming them with too much information too soon in the sales process.
- Adopt a five-part approach that works whether you are creating an email, voicemail, video, presentation, sales webpage, whitepaper, article, webinar or masterclass.
- Connect with an audience using narratives to acquire new customers on a small budget (reducing your Customer Acquisition Cost) and save time closing them.
- Learn how to sell more to existing customers and

keep the customers that you have so that you increase Customer Lifetime Value, even if you only have a single product at this point.

- Tailor your communication techniques and sales offers to anticipate and remove objections before your customer even realizes you are doing this, so that you close customers quickly.
- Refocus your messaging to what a purchase will mean to the customer personally and professionally, leaving them with the understanding that you care about them.

Put this to work immediately in your business by modeling the examples in this book. Action sheets will guide you through the process of customizing all of your communications to your specific message and purpose.

Why I Wrote this Book

During my 20 years in the enterprise and SAAS business, it has been my joy to serve customers and to give sales teams the tools and coaching they need to close business by communicating effectively with customers.

Whereas every product will be different in the way that you position it competitively, one thing remains constant....

Useful *and frequent* communication with the customer will open up new sales opportunities. It will grease the wheels to software license and subscription renewals, simply because your customers will know how you can help and that you care.

It became increasingly difficult to get my customers' attention amid "*email inbox overwhelm*" and their busy schedules. I struggled to get customers to take immediate action after a presentation, whitepaper download or webinar.

So, I had to tune my methods into those I write about in this book.

It was frustrating. As an engineer by background, I had to learn how to market and sell. And these techniques are not what they teach you at MBA school.

I learned the hard way that having a superior product compared with the current market leader does not mean that you will automatically win any deal.

I learned that having a product that you know the customer can benefit from does not mean they will listen, far from it: this is a lesson hard-learned as I managed an SAAS software "email customization" product line that eventually competed successfully against an industry gorilla, and then the introduction of new enterprise Computer-Aided Design tools that grew our portfolio and transaction sizes even though our customers had feared a high conversion cost if they were to adopt our solution over what they were currently using.

There is one more thing that you need to do to motivate a customer to pay attention, as you allay adoption fears.

The battle starts by being cognizant of the customer's emotions during the sales process, ranging from getting their attention at all, to making them understand they can win with what you offer. It involves taking care to remove lingering sales objections early so that you avoid chasing deals that lead nowhere.

You can do this by following a simple five-step framework to communicate a concept that gets attention, keeps it and leaves a lasting impression, driving customers onward to the next step.

You have probably been told to "develop rapport" and perform "value-based selling". This is a fantastic start... but it is insufficient to motivate the customer to take action so that you can close a sale.

Why do we remember a speech, want a cool set of shoes or gadget?

It's because of the vision created in the customer's mind of owning it. Specifically it is what owning it will say about who *he/she* is and who *we* are. Our *identity*. It's because of how we felt when we heard the speech's story; how it completely changed our mindset.

I will show you how to adapt your presentations, webinars, emails, voicemails, webpages, articles and whitepapers to focus *toward* the customer's emotional desire to buy, and *away* from price or, "I'm too busy", "It's too risky", "It won't work" excuses.

The methods that I am sharing allowed me to successfully compete with free software, retain software customers for a decade and counting, and generate eight figures annually from the purchased software.

It came from a mindset of caring about what my customers needed and wishing the very best for them, within the scope of growing my own businesses.

My wish for you is that, after you have read this book, customers will think of you as a "good vendor"; no, a great vendor; no, a *partner*; a company they want to adopt and continue to do business with.

Armed with what you apply from this book, I am confident that new communication channels with customers will open so that you can serve them, identify new sales opportunities and get paid what you are worth.

Let's get started!

PART 1

Noticed And Remembered

"A business absolutely devoted to service will have only one thing to worry about: profits. They will be embarrassingly large."

— Henry Ford

Chapter 1

Why People Ignore You And How To Fix It

"Writing persuasively is not about persuasion. It's about empathy."

— Ray Edwards (Direct response copywriter)

"As you grow older, you will discover that you have two hands, one for helping yourself, the other for helping others."

— Audrey Hepburn

Curiosity, Insecurity And Fear

The ad below, created by Max Sackheim, first appeared in a newspaper in 1921.

Do You Make These Mistakes in English?

It was so successful that it ran for 40 years.

Why was it so successful?

To answer that question, let me ask you this.
When you read it, do you become immediately curious about the answer to the question?
Do you then start to wonder whether your own command of the English language is correct and effective?
The ad created curiosity.
But there is more to it than that.The tone of the question exudes *authority* ... which amplifies the reader's curiosity.

And there is one other thing going on here.

The ad taps into reader *emotions* of fear and insecurity. Not in a bad way, yet in a way that makes the reader wonder even more whether they might benefit from brushing up their English.

When you read this headline, it does one thing. It taps emotions that make you read on. You are HOOKED !!

Simplicity

When you go out and sell the product, what objections might a customer have to buying?
For Max's ad, the sales objections might be, "It's hard work to learn better English" ... "I don't have the time" ....
"Does your product even work?"
The ad addresses these objections upfront by emphasizing the solution's simplicity. It states that 100,000 users successfully used it ... and it took them just 15 minutes per day.
This reassures the audience that they will get a *result* easily.

Well, shut my mouth and call me hungry!

Connection And Empathy

Dove, a manufacturer of soap and other beauty products, ran the video ad below.

Their *"You are more beautiful than you think"* ad connects with its audience via something that most men and women feel … low self-esteem.

In the ad, each woman describes her face to a sketch artist. You gain empathy for her as she struggles to come up with words to describe herself.
The artist creates two sketches, one on the basis of how she described herself.
The other from her actual face as he sees it.

The two sketches are compared.

In the first week that the ad was released it gained over 20 million shares. The number of views on YouTube alone is, as of late 2021, in excess of 60 million.

Why is this ad so effective? Because it empathizes with how the audience feels about themselves …. and gives them hope.

When you are *good listener* and when you *look for the emotions underlying a customer's response*, you practice empathy.

Dove Real Beauty Sketches | You're more beautiful than you think (3mins)

69,617,870 views • Apr 14, 2013

Dove US
148K subscribers

Pleasure, Humor and Happiness

Why does this meme make its audience of dog owners laugh and remember it?

WHAT MAKES YOU FEEL POWERFUL?

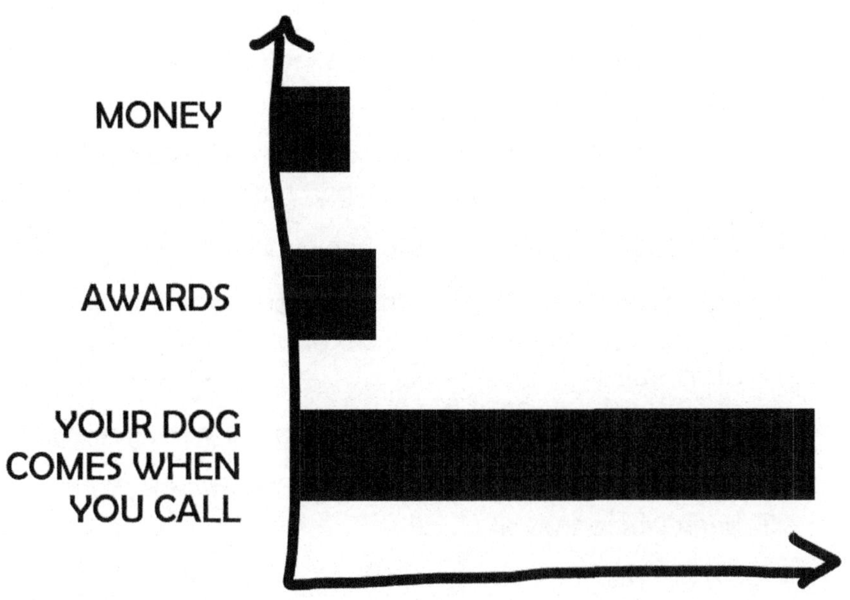

First, it has a humorous twist to it, which creates the emotion of happiness.

And then it resonates with dog lovers about how immensely pleasureful it feels when their dog responds positively to them.

The point?

Find things in common with your audience that will make them smile. They will like you because they feel as though you understand them.

Summary

People will be interested in buying and will remember you, not because of what you say but instead because of how you make them *feel*.

People buy on emotion.

The feelings that drive toward a sale include the emotions of:

- **EMPATHY** – The feeling that you understand and sympathize with them
- **PAIN** – How they feel about a burning problem that they need to fix, that you can help them fix
- **PLEASURE** (Humor and Happiness) – A vision of how great things will be after they purchase
- **CURIOSITY** - They want to know more.
- **FEAR and INSECURITY** that something bad might happen, or the FEAR of Missing Out (FOMO) if they don't buy
- **SIMPLICITY –** The reassurance that they will get results
- **CONNECTION** – They feel that you care and, "You've been where they are."

This book will teach you to use these exact communication emotions that drive sales.

It will show you exactly how to structure your communications – your emails, presentations, whitepapers, articles, webinars and masterclasses, voicemails and sales web pages — in order to get your audience's attention, keep it, and drive them to a next step in the sales process.

Chapter 2

I Wanted It Before You Showed It To Me

"You have got to start with the customer experience and work backwards to the technology....
Where can we take the customer?
You don't need to know anything about what's in the box".

—Steve Jobs

Is Selling A Chore?

I twisted my ankle the first weekend of June 2014, so I sat down, religiously “elevating and icing” the ankle amid the peace and quiet of my home, dogs at my side.

Was I bothered? Nope. In fact, this represented a great opportunity to write the “killer whitepaper” that had been on my mind for over a month.

I loved to “geek out” on my semiconductor design tool product line, given my engineering background, and rarely had time to do so now that I was responsible for its entire business success.

For my company, whitepapers were one of the best ways to gain qualified and targeted leads.

When well-written, whitepapers set you apart. You become the resident expert in your chosen topic.

And this particular whitepaper did indeed generate highly targeted leads, which led to software product evaluations and sales.

But then something surprising happened.

About 80% of these super enthused customers that were evaluating our software went “radio silent” on us. They would not return our calls.

What Can You Do To Drive A Sale?

Why does what looks like a “shoo-in” sales evaluation die on the vine?

Why the deathly silence from the customer? They would not respond to our emails.... or return our phone calls. All this after having been in a rush to get started.

The same goes for your existing customers. Why is it that they fail to call us back when we contact them with the offer of help?

The truth is that your customer or prospect is overwhelmed with their existing to-do lists and easily bored with material being sent to them day in, day out.
Yet, here's the irony. The same customer is not too busy to watch a 90-minute movie... or engage in a 15-minute "water cooler" conversation.
The answer to the question of how to get a response boils down to this:

> You need to prime the sale. That is, you need to make them want your offer, emotionally, before you ever start any evaluation.

I will show you how in this chapter.

You will learn to:

1. Get and keep customer attention
2. Motivate customers to initiate an action that moves them closer to the sale

Priming a sale will be one of your biggest time savers.

If you are constantly presenting and bombarding customers with information about your software's features and benefits before you have primed the sale, know this...

You're too early !!

If you are launching into a software evaluation or trial period before you prime the sale ...

You're too early !!

And what's worse?
Even if the evaluation moves forward, unless you prime the sale, you are more than likely going to have to deal with the customer grumbling :

- "It's too expensive"
- "It's too risky"
- "I don't have the time."
- "I don't think it will work."

First Make Customers EMOTIONALLY WANT Your Product

How should you prime the sale?

That is, how can you make the customer emotionally want your product before they even know what it is?

Do these three things *before* you waste time on an evaluation:

1. *Empathize* with the customer's pain .. so they feel you understand their situation and really care.

   "I've been there, too."

   "That must really be tough."

2. *Amplify* their pain…so they understand that "doing nothing" is not an option.

   "How would you feel a year from now if you still had that *pain*?"

   "Why do you think that you haven't solved this yet?"

   "How does that pain make you feel?"

3. *Paint A Vision* of how it will feel to have solved the problem.

   "Here's the transformation that happened to (me/

> customer) when I used (product) and how I felt."
> "Enjoy the luxury that you deserve"

In its strongest form, the vision is the *identity* that your product might give your customer. For example, Nike's *"Just Do It"* campaign that makes you assume an identity of empowerment.

Let's discuss how to show empathy, to amplify pain and then paint a vision.

Find The "Pain"

How exactly do we elicit the customer's pain?

That is, make our customer tell us about it and the scale of its impact on them?

Let's look at an example.

Perhaps your customer states this about your product:

"It's too expensive"....

And you feel compelled to respond like this

> "Hmmm... If you don't mind me asking... Could you help me better understand why you believe that it's too expensive?"

Quite often, the rookie salesperson will stop there as the customer proceeds to explain why they can't afford it and that, by the way, your competitor charges less.

The problem?

The rookie is now talking about price (bad), instead of pain (good).

And the sale stalls.

The experienced sales professional instead diagnoses the customer's problems until they find PAIN.

> "Tell me what bothers you about your current solution."
> "What keeps you up at night?"
> And… "Why is that?"

Once you have found the pain, ask ….

> "Tell me what it would mean to you personally and professionally if you could solve this problem."
>
> Boom! PAIN and what it means to the customer to fix it have now been uncovered!!

Empathize With And Amplify Emotional Pain

The customer's answer has now shifted to the PAIN they are experiencing

For example:

- Nail-biting schedule delays
- Worry that their competitors will beat them to market
- Concern that their staff is stressed, working overtime using the current approach
- Fear that their own customers will jump ship

The next step is to AMPLIFY the pain by talking about the **toll it takes on your customer.**

To discover the emotional cost of the pain, you might say ….

> "That sounds like a real challenge. Tell me more about the (PAIN) you feel."
>
> "I have been in your exact situation. Tell me, what worries you most about (PAIN). **What does it stop you from doing?"**

> "How would it make you feel if you still had (PAIN) a year from now?"
>
> "That's terrible. What will happen if you don't get rid of (PAIN)?"

I once wrote a whitepaper whose main title was "No Room For Error." It was about creating the highly-reliable (mission-critical) semiconductors used in outer space, where failure can be life-threatening.
Consider a similar frame for your customer.

Ask them "**What's the COST OF A MISTAKE?"**

Do this and your customer will realize they need to fix their "pain".

Paint The Vision

What does your solution mean to the customer, personally and professionally? More importantly, **how will your product make your customer feel?**

They might feel:

- **Safe** in the knowledge that there will be minimal schedule delays
- **Happy** to now have the means to beat competitors to market
- **Glad** that staff will go home and be with their families early instead of sweating over countless tasks at the office late at night
- **Confident** that they will see predictable revenue growth from an expanding customer base
- **A New Identity - They might now feel sophisticated, empowered**

This feeling is the vision that you want to instill in the customer in order to sell to them.

To discover the customer's vision, you can ask ....

"*How would you feel* if you could solve (PAIN)?"

"What would solving (PAIN) mean that you can achieve and *why does that matter to you*?"

"Where would you like your business/status to be one year from now and *how would that feel*?"

Do this and let the customer visualize receiving the end result that your solution promises.

This book will show you how to use STORIES to establish empathy, amplify pain, and create a vision to eliminate it.

Summary

I learnt to prime the sale using emotional language that made my customers realize that they needed our product. Priming involved empathizing, amplifying the pain, and creating a vision of how great life would be once the pain had gone away.

When I did this, four things happened:

1. We stopped wasting time on evaluations destined to go nowhere. If the customer responded to our pain amplification questions, we knew we had a good prospect that truly was in pain.
2. Customers called us back. With an open communication channel created upfront with the customer, we had visibility to help the customer succeed in their evaluation.
3. Customers felt comfortable working with us because we had shown them that we cared.
4. We shifted the frame of discussion away from price, to fixing their pain:
   "This is how we can help you."

You can do this, too!

I will show you an exact framework that achieves this for each customer communication — whether it's an email, voicemail, presentation, webinar, masterclass, video, whitepaper or article

Chapter 3

Drive Customers To Take Action .... Now!

Without Action, Nothing Changes

—Tony Robbins

"I'm all in ! I am good at breaking things," I told my software team as they were looking for people to beta test our software.

I like to press *all* the buttons, select *all* the menu options… because I am curious to see what they can do for me ...

I am not alone in my addiction to buying and using new software.

But let's step back for a minute and look at what underlies someone's willingness to participate in any project.

To want your software

And want to act now.

What Makes Customers Take Action…*Right Now*?!

Some of our sales engagements would drag on at the pace of a snail for months….

So, I came up with purposeful ways to move the sales process along quickly.

What will make a customer feel as though they need to take action? For example open an email, respond to your voicemail, complete their software evaluation, buy?
There are, in fact, five things.

1. **MOTIVATION**

   You do something that *Gets Their Attention* – You "**HOOK**" them, with a clever headline, for example.

   I will teach you how to write headlines in this book.

   You tell a **STORY** that relates to their own personal emotions and pain.

And, at the end of it all, you use the story to remove doubts that your SOLUTION addresses their objections and fears.

2. They **EXPERIENCE EMPATHY** - the fact that you care.

   "Did the customer think this when they heard from me?"

   - This vendor "gets me!"
   - This vendor "has my back!"

   A well-crafted "story" will portray the empathy that you have.

3. **DEADLINE**

   "There is nothing like the last minute to get something done!"
   Often called "urgency", a deadline forces a decision of "yes" or "no" by a particular date and time.
   What will often inspire that elusive "yes" is **fear of missing out (FOMO)** on some kind of time-limited bonus or special offer.

   The deadline is expressed as a **"CALL TO ACTION"** such as "Purchase before this date".

4. **ABILITY (CONFIDENCE)**

   The customer is crystal clear on the action that they need to take, by when ...and why.
   Express this using a **SINGLE (ONE) KEY TAKEAWAY** within your communication... And, yes, I mean just one !!

   But there is another component to this that will reassure the customer.

   The customer is likely to take action if they are confident that you have a solution that will get them a RESULT that they want.

An **OFFER** that includes line items such as "24/7 customer support", "templates", "cheat sheets", "compatibility modes", goes a long way to allay any fear of change or of a steep learning curve.

5. A **TRIGGER** that activates the customer to take action at the precise time that they need your solution. Examples of triggers include:
    - A reminder or follow-up message
    - Frequent communication with your customer such as weekly emails, so that, at the exact time that they need help, they think of you

In the next chapter, you will learn a framework to communicate. A method that addresses every single one of these motivations, so that you drive customers in the direction of a purchase.

We will use the "Sell Bigger" Framework.

Summary

Customers come in many shapes and sizes, but they have one thing in common – Fear; fear that freezes them in their tracks, that actually creates distress. Fear that prevents them from taking the one action that would better themselves.

Customers are driven to take your suggested next step in the sales process by:

- Motivation – You hooked them with your headline and told them a story that made them emotionally want what you offer.
- Experiencing for themselves that you care
- A deadline by which they must make a decision, else lose out (FOMO)
- Confidence in their ability to succeed – which you can communicate with one key takeaway in your email and then reinforce via your offer
- A trigger that reminds them to take action, such as frequent communications that remind them of their pain, follow up messages that remind that you can help

In the next chapter, you are going to learn how to use a communication framework, the

"SELL BIGGER FRAMEWORK" to drive your customers into action.

PART 2

How To Structure Every Communication

The only way a relationship will last
is if you see your relationship as a place that you go to
give, and not where you go to take

—Tony Robbins

The "SELL BIGGER FRAMEWORK" is a communication system that stops people from ignoring you and gets them instead to pay attention and take action...

....be it an email, webinar, presentation, masterclass, video, voicemail, whitepaper, article, journal, landing page, or "online sales funnel".

When you implement this framework, you will:

- LOOK DIFFERENT
  That is, when your customer is faced with a full inbox or is perusing a webpage, your particular communication will jump out at them
  How?
  A "**Pattern Interrupt"** will be used to make you stand out so that your audience clicks on your email headline in their cluttered inbox or is drawn to your video on a webpage.

- GET IMMEDIATE ATTENTION
  How? By crafting an attention-grabbing headline or **"Hook"** that makes people notice and open an email, listen to a presentation... or click on your articles and videos.

- KEEP ATTENTION
  How? By using a "**Story**"

- LEAVE A LASTING IMPRESSION
  How? By listing **One Key Takeaway**

- TELL CUSTOMERS WHAT TO DO NEXT
  Why they should act now - a strong **Call To Action or Offer**

When we put it all together, it looks like this!

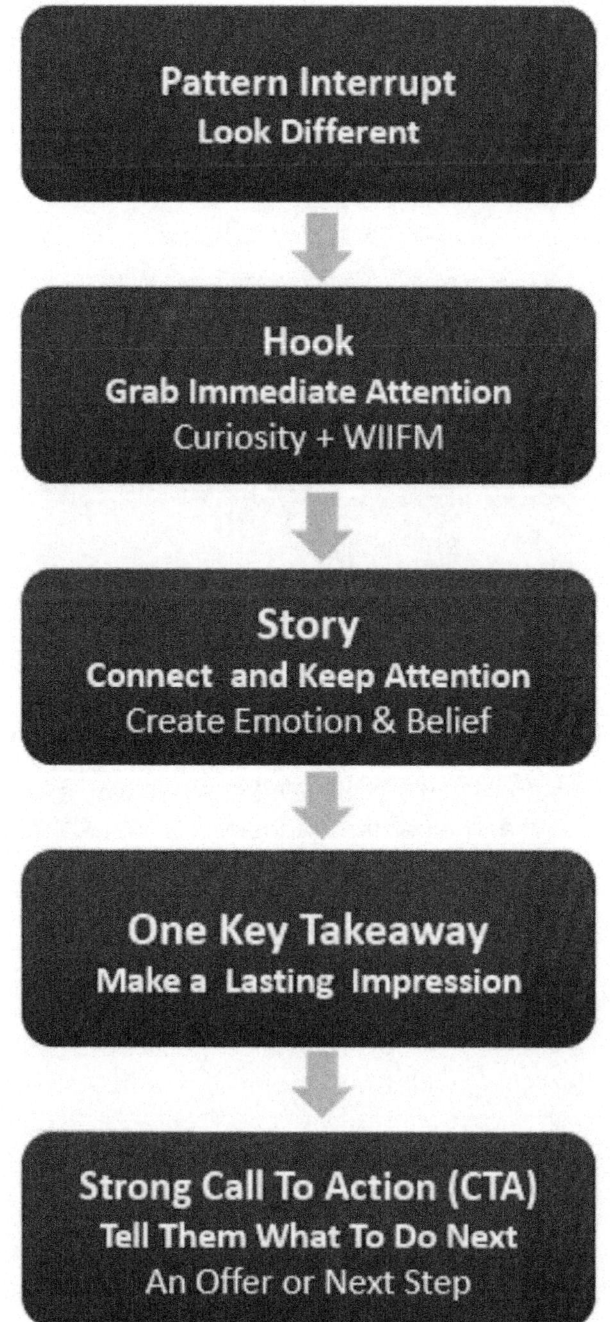

Let's look at each of these steps to understand how to use them in your own communications...

In your voicemails, emails, presentations, webinars/master-classes, videos, sales webpages, white papers and articles.

Looking Different

Do you remember the company *America Online* ("AOL")?

Once upon a time, in the early 1990s, email was a novel convenience... and a game-changer!

I remember looking forward to each email; a dozen or so landing in my business inbox daily.

And then AOL produced an email service for the home consumer; I could send and receive information instantly.

An end to wrestling with the buttons of a temperamental Fax machine.
Not to mention that email was "night and day" faster than printing out a letter and sending it via "snail mail".

Yet, today, the following is how I think about email... and perhaps you do, too?

"I dread logging in every morning because I know that I'll be greeted with 100 new unread emails, half of them leaving me wondering how the sender got my address in the first place. Many lurk in my inbox unopened.
In fact, I have tens of thousands of unopened emails.

Sifting through them every day sucks up my time and distracts me."

Yes, I have *Inbox Overwhelm*.

Adding to the pressure exerted by my ever-expanding Inbox are deadlines to meet, colleagues to call, the dog barking and a meeting to prepare for at 4pm. Sheesh!

Let me introduce you to an overloaded, stressed, and distracted customer, who, just like you and I, has not enough hours in the day.
You have no idea how much else is going on in his or her life, but you can likely guess how busy he or she is.

Which leads to my point:

You take hours to write emails, compose helpful webinars and videos, yet the chances are quite good that your customer will never read (let alone act) on any of them.

The stakes involved in getting a customer to read *and act* are huge.

Customers will read, watch, listen to a chosen few emails. Why is that?

It starts first with *getting their attention*, no small feat; yet a feat offering a chance to connect...and sell.

It's for this reason that we are now going to explore two attention-grabbing techniques...

the "PATTERN INTERRUPT" and the "HOOK".

Once the customer's attention is garnered, we will keep it with a "STORY", and make one memorable point with a "ONE KEY TAKEAWAY".

We will then drive to a sale with a "CALL TO ACTION" and an "OFFER".

So, How Do We Get Their Attention?!!

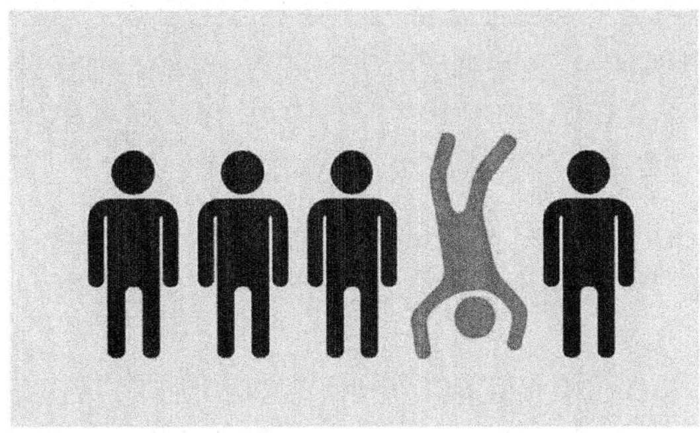

What's the one and only purpose of an email subject line...an article title, or a video thumbnail?

The answer: Its job, and *only job,* is to stop the customer in their tracks and get them to click .... even when the audience feels they are too busy and overwhelmed.

The email subject line, article title and video thumbnail are the single most important details to get right. They are what gets customers to consume what you communicate.

If customers are not consuming your content, the first thing to look at changing is the headline or thumbnail.

Let me ask you something.

When was the last time you spent more than a minute composing your email's headline...or thought about how your video might catch someone's eye?

You are not alone in perhaps simply blowing through this process in your haste to get your communication out the door.

So how should we grab attention?

Why, with "**Pattern Interrupts**" and **"Hooks"**!

- **Something that catches the eye and stops the scroll, perhaps a video thumbnail or an emoji, is called a "PATTERN INTERRUPT".** Examples include a quantified number or something on tire.
- **We call the video thumbnail, title, subject line or headline a "HOOK",** since it gives the viewer a reason to click.

Let's look, in detail, at how to construct hooks and pattern interrupts.

Chapter 4

The Pattern Interrupt "Look Different"

"The only league to be in is the league of your own"

—Angela Sutton

The Sell Bigger Framework

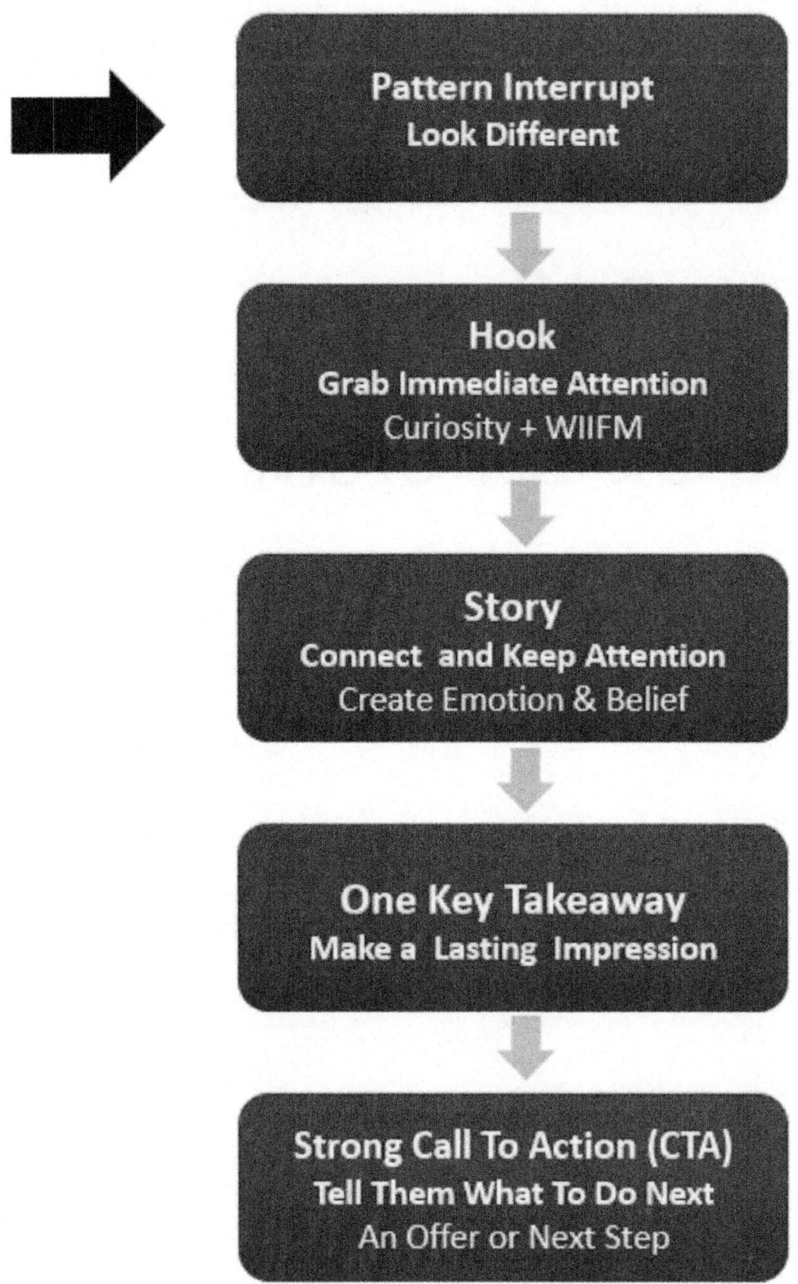

The Five-Second Rule

My company was exhibiting with a large trade show booth at the Consumer Electronics Show in Las Vegas.

The day before the show, there was a short training session that taught us how best to strike up a conversation with folks who might be strolling past our booth on the show floor. The attention-grabbing technique came down to this:

We had just five seconds to attract a potential customer as he or she walked by.

What did we need to convey in those five seconds?

- First – WIIFM (What's In It For Me?). Our signage, in large letters, told passers-by why they personally should care about what we were selling.
- Second – CURIOSITY. Our signage asked questions that made them stop and think and then immediately want to know more.
- Third - LOOK DIFFERENT – We needed to stand out. For this, we chose to amuse our customers. We hired a magician. Someone who fascinated them enough that they wanted to stop for a moment in order to look and laugh.

These same three entities are necessary in *any* communication.

Curiosity and WIIFM are created in the headline. A Pattern Interrupt, when used, will make you stand out even more because it will make you look different

So, what exactly is a "pattern interrupt"?

It's an extra something to grab the customer's attention, ... to stop viewers from scrolling by on the screen, amid noisy news feeds, or from missing your message amid pages of unread emails, a full voicemail box, or other distractions. The PATTERN INTERRUPT merely makes sure that the customer sees your title or subject line (HOOK) in the first place.

It's the sore thumb  or the glitter  that stands out!

Pattern Interrupt Examples

Here are some Email pattern interrupt examples:

- An Emoji
  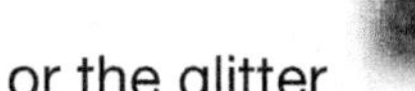"Five ways to get prospects to call you back."
- A power word such as "FREE" in caps.
  "A vs. B – Which is better? Download FREE report."
- A quantified number:
  "My customer cut cost-of-goods by 27% using this one trick."
- Benefit or gift in square brackets:
  "[PDF Attached]: Your design blueprint."
- A shocking or controversial statement:
  "You are poor because you are perfect".

Here are some video pattern interrupt examples:

- A human waving
- A camera zooming in and out quickly
- A high or low camera filming angle

- An alarming or unusual prop, such as something on fire …
- A fast object or person running across the screen
- A glitchy, shaky video
- Puppies or babies
- A funny facial expression
- The words "TURN UP THE SOUND" superimposed over the video

Once we have garnered attention with the pattern interrupt, we will fascinate our customer some more with our headline or video thumbnail. The "Hook".

Summary

Your communication has a lot in common with my trade show booth at the Las Vegas trade show.

Your email or video has a split second to stand out from the crowd in a way that makes it cause you to pause. It must look different from the crowd.

The way to do this is to use a pattern interrupt.

This chapter shows you how to create email and video pattern interrupts.

For emails, a pattern interrupt might be an emoji, power word such as "FREE", a quantified number, square brackets in the title, or a shocking statement

For videos, a pattern interrupt might be something that naturally appeals to people such as motion, a puppy, it may be some unusual shaking in the video or it could be a strange filming angle.

Chapter 5

The Hook “Grab Immediate Attention”

“Change is made by people who show up”

—Rep. Jamie Raskin

The Sell Bigger Framework

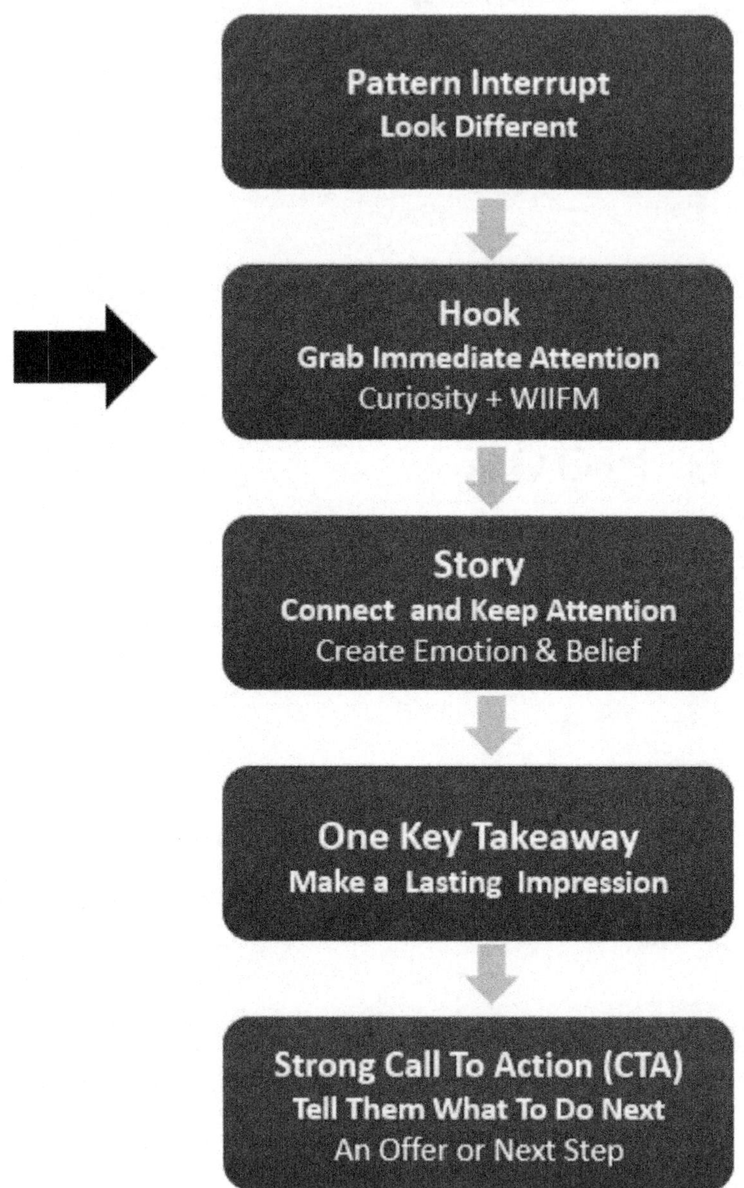

Beethoven's 5th symphony has a signature four-beat opening:

—"da da da daaaah".

You can't help but sit up in your seat when you hear it.

It dominates any other noise in the room.

And that four-beat theme recurs throughout the course of the entire symphony.

It shows up again and again, in variations of increasing textural complexity and emotional power.

It modulates, and shifts from major to minor keys.

You hear it so often that, by the end of the symphony, it's impossible to erase it from your brain ...
In other words, it becomes "catchy" and "unforgettable".

What can we learn from our friend Beethoven ?
In an era of distractions and inbox overwhelm, you will be heard if you create something that latches onto and grabs your customer's attention, just short of psychosis – A HOOK.

What exactly is a "hook"?

A hook is a HEADLINE, OPENING or TITLE.
A hook makes viewers want to know more, and therefore:

- Click to OPEN an email, article or white paper
- Click PLAY on a video or Podcast
- SIGN UP for a webinar/masterclass

A "hook" is your:

- Email subject line
- Video title

- Webinar/masterclass/presentation title
- Article or whitepaper heading
- First sentence of your voicemail

The Hook's sole purpose is to get the audience to click, watch or listen.

TIP: If people are not responding to your emails, the first thing to change is the hook.

What Are The Ingredients Of A Great Hook?

The hook (headline, title, opening) needs to do at least one of these two things:

1. Spark CURIOSITY
2. Strongly portray a WIIFM (What's In It For Me?) to your customer

The two magical ingredients of a great hook are:
Curiosity + WIIFM
(Use at least one)

Look at some of your recent email subject lines or presentation titles and ask yourself whether they do either of these two things.

If not, here's what to do:

To understand how to create a great hook, let's first look at what you want your customer to *feel* after they read the HOOK.

You will generally want to pick one of three things that you want them to feel:

1. "I want the answer to that question."

   Hook examples:

   a. Do you make these mistakes when designing an integrated circuit?
   b. Classic Design vs. Modern Design – Which works better in 2021?

2. "I want to know more."

   Hook examples:

   a. What do the top 1% of circuit designers do that the other 99% don't?
   b. Having a perfect product will ruin your business.

3. "I need to know what happens next" (A Cliffhanger).

   Hook examples:

   a. How my lousy presentation led my customer to buy $1M more than they had planned.
   b. A little mistake that cost my software customer $30,000...per year.

How To Find Your Hook

A good first way to find a hook is to consider your customer's *WIIFM*, for example a question or cliffhanger that would make them *curious*... Like this:

Your customer's WIIFM is the ...

- *Emotion* or *pain* they feel
- *Result* or ROI they seek
- *Roadblock* they face (a sales objection, myth or false belief)
- *Problem* they want to avoid
- *Promise* that will be fulfilled if they click or watch

Things that will make your customer *curious* include:

- An unexpected occurrence ... such as point of *high drama* in your story
- How you will *compare and contrast* two issues or products

After viewing the examples that follow, fill out the action sheet to create your own hook.

Hook Examples

The emotion or pain felt is the hook:

(This kind of hook appeals to your customer's identity. The emotional word is shown in *italics*).

- I was *afraid* of filming a video of myself, until I tried this.
- How I overcame customer *anxiety* when I delivered their new software five weeks late.
- The *danger* of not addressing customer complaints quickly, even when you disagree with them
- Why it's a *bad* idea to get up early
- Why I *hate* the status-quo in graphic design
- You became a designer because you wanted to *make a difference*

Your hook is the *result* or ROI that customer will see:

- Format: How to get (results) within (the allowed time frame) even with (massive excuses)
    - o E.g., How to create stunning graphics for your slides in less than 10 minutes, even if you are not technically-inclined
- Format: The one thing that my customer did to get results within (timeframe) without (fear/excuses)

- E.g., The one thing my customer did to completely analyze their design in less than 10 minutes without ever having to read the software manual

- Format: How to get (results) without (fear) even if (excuse)
  - E.g., "How to write a whitepaper without any copywriting experience, even if you already have a 60 hour work week."

To pre-sell an offer, you will often want to build a special bond or connection with the customer through shared experiences.

You will also want to create *new beliefs* that persuade them to buy, overcoming their objections.

Here are some hooks to use with each of these types of communication.

The hook is the customer's roadblock or problem they want to avoid:

Fill in the words in brackets to suit your need:

- Format: How to overcome problem without (pain/objection) even if (excuse/fear)
  - E.g., How to overcome stage fright without much practice or creating a script, even if you have never presented before.
- Format: The real cause of (roadblock)
  - E.g., The real cause of insomnia
- Format: The real reason you have (problem) and what to do about it
  - E.g., The real reason that product schedules slip and what to do about it

Headlines that create a *connection* with your customer are very effective here.

For example:

- Format: You became a (your profession) because you wanted to (solve this Problem)
    - E.g., You started your business because you believe that customers shouldn't have to feel overwhelmed and lost.
- Format: What I do to (solve problem/overcome roadblock)
    - E.g., What I do to overcome writer's block.
    - E.g., What I do to maintain life balance.

The promise is the hook:

A "Promise" hook is great for a webinar or masterclass.

Fill in the words in capitals to suit your need:

1. Watch till the end and I will show you how to get access to (thing they want) for free
2. Don't buy (product) until you read this
3. Does (product/approach) really solve (problem) ?
4. How my ugly email brought $1.7M of new business in one day

The point of high drama is the hook:

Take the high-drama or most intriguing part of your email or presentation's story and use it as the headline to draw customers in

1. I was about to kill my development project, and then I thought, "What if I did *this* instead?"
2. I never thought that I would lose the sale, and then *this* happened.
3. How a split-second decision to record and automate my colleague's coding tasks saved my business.

An unexpected occurrence or point of high drama in your story is the hook:

Fill in the words in (brackets) to suit your need:

- Format: (main character) gets (turning point)
    - E.g., Steve gets amnesia and forgets to check in with his customer
    - E.g., Bart gets trolled
- Format: The (trait) (role)
    - E.g., The accidental engineer
- Format: (Main character's) redemption
    - E.g., Prince Harry's redemption
- Format: (Story theme) in (location)
    - E.g., Cliffhanger in Silicon Valley
- Format: The (villain) and (main character or object)
    - E.g., The engineer and the unreliable server farm
- Format: A Farewell to (main character or thing)
    - E.g., A Farewell to Old School marketing
- Format: An old (technique) that is used even more today
    - E.g., An old copywriting tactic from the 1930's that works even better today in digital marketing

The hook compares and contrasts two issues or products:

One way to think about this is how your *big idea* might you help the customer form a *New Belief* that overcomes an objection (or myth).

Fill in the words in brackets to suit your need:

1. Format: Doing (old way) is the biggest mistake that any business can make.
2. Format: The one small process change that had the biggest impact on my software business
3. Format: Why (old way) was costing my telecom customer $50K/day...and what they did to fix it.
4. Format: Not adapting *your* software marketing solution is costing money and time.
5. Format: (Option 1) vs. (Option 2) – Which is better?

Use the action sheet on the next page to create your hook.

Hook Action Sheet

- STEP 1 – Hook Ideas -

By looking at the story and message of your communication, fill out any of the boxes in the following form with ideas.
Mark whether the idea creates WIIFM or Curiosity

		WIIFM?	Curiosity
PAIN OR EMOTION FELT		☐	☐
RESULT/ROI		☐	☐
ROADBLOCK		☐	☐
PROBLEM		☐	☐
PROMISE		☐	☐
UNEXPECTED OCCURRENCE OR POINT OF HIGH DRAMA		☐	☐
COMPARE & CONTRAST		☐	☐

- STEP 2 – Create your HOOK -

MY HOOK ...

- ❑ ANSWERS A QUESTION
- ❑ MAKES PEOPLE "WANT TO KNOW"
- ❑ IS A CLIFFHANGER

MY HOOK IS:

Summary

We can take a lesson from Beethoven's 5th symphony in the way that its opening bars grab our attention.

In an era of distractions and inbox overwhelm, you too can be heard when you create a headline that grabs your customer's attention.

You can do this using a "hook".

The hook's sole purpose is to get the audience to click, watch or listen.

In an email, video, presentation, whitepaper or article, the hook is the title or headline.
In a voicemail, it's the first sentence that you utter.

Great hooks use at least one of these 2 things

- WIIFM (What's in it for me)
- Curiosity (I want to know the answer to a question, I want to know more, I want to know what happens next)

Your customer's WIIFM is the ...*emotion* or *pain* they feel, *result* or ROI they seek, *roadblock* they face (a sales objection, myth or false belief), *problem* they want to avoid or *promise* that will be fulfilled if they click or watch.

Things that will make your customer *curious* include an unexpected occurrence or how your communication will *compare and contrast* two issues or products.

This chapter contains a plethora of examples.

If customers are not responding to your communications, the first thing to fix is the hook.

The hook matters more than any other piece of the communication, because it is what determines whether your communication will be consumed or not.

Chapter 6

The Story "Connect and Keep Attention "

"People don't think in terms of information.
They think in terms of narratives.
But while people focus on the story itself, information comes along for the ride."

—Jonah Berger—From the book, "*Contagious*"

The Sell Bigger Framework

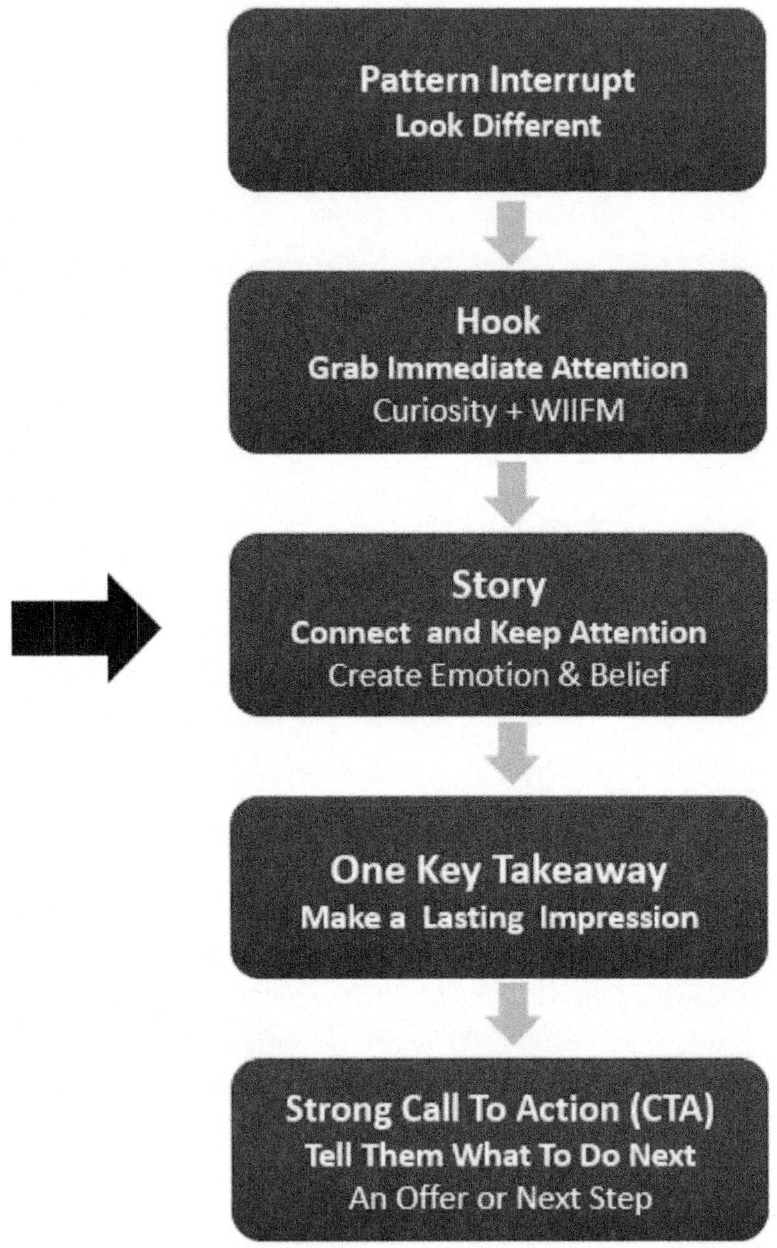

In co-founder of Apple Inc., Steve Jobs' biography, Walter Isaacson describes the day that Jobs was reviewing a prototype of the MacIntosh Computer.

Jobs was unhappy with how slowly the Mac started up (it's "boot" time).

Jobs challenged the lead engineer working on the Mac Operating System to get the Mac to boot (start up) 10 seconds faster.

But there was a problem.

The engineer insisted that it was impossible. And he truly believed this to be the case.

So, Jobs asked him a question,

"If it would save a person's life, could you shave 10 seconds off the boot time?"

Jobs went to a whiteboard and demonstrated the following...

"If five million users booted up their Mac every day 10 seconds faster, then that amounted to 300 million hours saved. That is the equivalent of 100 lifetimes saved per week."

The moral of this story?

Like Jobs, you can motivate people by guiding them to see a bigger picture.

Jobs created a *vision of how things could be* and *why it mattered.*

Painting the bigger picture is just one example of what you can accomplish when you tell a story.

Think about a presentation you attended, that you remember as though it were yesterday...

... that made you want to act immediately.

... that changed how you thought about a problem.

... that improved your understanding.

Why was that?

Did the presentation spark an *emotion* inside of you?

Perhaps it was a customer testimonial? Perhaps the story of someone who didn't stand a prayer and yet beat the odds? Perhaps a tale that included a funny story?

The reason why these presentations stick around in your brain long after you see them is that they make you *feel* something emotionally.

The lesson?

People remember how you made them *feel*.

When you instill a *vision* of how things could be in a customer's mind, it will spark emotions that include happiness and excitement ... And the customer will remember you because of it.

FBI Negotiator Jim Camp negotiated with kidnappers.
How did he succeed?
He would paint a *vision* of what it would mean to the kidnapper ... and what they could do... after the hostage was released.

... His mantra ...

"No VISION, No ACTION"

A sale is no different. When you create a vision for your customer, it will also help you to close a sale!!

How do you create a vision in your customer's mind with a story?

Your story might, for example, describe what was going through your mind when you encountered the same situation that the customer now finds themself in (how you felt).

Sound daunting?

I will show you exactly how to find your story and then tell it in the natural way that a customer will love.
But first, consider the customer's reaction when you present a set of features and benefits in a presentation.

Then compare this with the reaction you get when you showcase a live example or **case study story** that describes what it meant to the customer to gain success with your product.

The key is to *capture within your story what your product* means to a customer. How it makes them feel.

As an example, consider how you feel when you watch Shark Tank on TV, and hear a story about why someone was driven to create their company to help others avoid a personal disaster that had happened to someone they loved.
Your eyes might well up with tears when you hear these stories.
The thing to realize is that *your* company too has a story behind its origin – An **origin story.**

An origin story can, for example, convey a problem that you had that you solved. This happens to be the very same problem, and a result that the customer longs for.

How can you adapt your emails to now include a story …. so that the recipient reads and remembers them?

It's not as hard as you think.

Let me give you an example.

Suppose for a moment that you are writing an email that communicates a tip.
The tip answers a frequently asked question for the project planning software that you sell – The answer to that very question sits on the software's user manual

Instead of just answering the question in your email, you decide to take a photo of yourself staring at the copy of the user manual on the computer screen.
You send this picture to your friend with a message:

> "Hey - I was just helping a customer to answer this question (list the question).
>
> The answer was in Chapter 7 of the user manual and I thought that you might be interested in it. The answer is ___"

Immediately, your answer becomes more memorable; simply because you *prefaced it with a story* about how you discovered the answer in the user manual.

The photo that you included imprints in your audience's mind a picture of the story, making it all the more memorable

Include a story often enough in your communications and the customer will indeed feel like they know you and think of you as a "good vendor" who cares about them.

Let's write down your *story* ideas using the action sheet.

Story Ideas Action Sheet

If you think you don't have a story, worry not!!
Things that happen in your life every day make for great stories.
Use the Action Sheet below to inspire one or more story ideas.

1. **A high or low point in my life** -- Fear, loss, pain, gain, stress
2. **A life-changing moment** or a **"moment of enlightenment"**
3. **How I beat the odds, turned a major setback into success and overcame my fears**
4. **What someone did that inspired ... and changed my perspective**

WHAT IS YOUR STORY'S PURPOSE?

a. If you were to Mentor a group, what one thing does your story teach them? Was there a moral to the story?

b. I could use this story when I want to talk about...

- ❑ Our Company's Origin
- ❑ A Case Study
- ❑ My Product
- ❑ Overcoming An Objection
- ❑ Shows Why I Care - I Want To Create Instant Connection
- ❑ A Key Point That I Want To Frame ... And Make Memorable

If you still struggle to find new stories, use one of these approaches:

- **Ask your customers to tell you about their greatest "roadblock"** – A challenge that they faced when trying to manually solve a big problem that they now solve by using your product .
- **Have a routine to, at the end and during the day, compile personal and work stories** . Log them in a story vault using an online tool such as Trello.

  Your dog, family, friend or customer do something funny?

  Write about it.

  Did you learn a lesson today when something went wrong?
  Write about it.

  Create a day-end debrief where you describe what went well ... and what didn't, and what you learned. These items can become great stories.

- **Post on social media a post "ASK ME ANYTHING ABOUT ___" about the topic that your company specializes in.**

  Or send a survey to your customer mailing list with this single question,
  "What burning questions about (topic) do you have that you would like me to answer?"

  Once you get a response, create a story about customers that had the same question. "Fred asked me this question __ "

- **Gather Frequently Asked Questions and then answer them**
  For example

"(Firstname) asked (question). This question comes up a lot because of (Story) ... Here's the answer ___"

- **Re-use an informational social media post that resulted in quite a popular reaction**
  Create a story, thus:

  "I posted information about (topic), thinking that it might be useful to my customers. To my surprise, this is what happened ___. This is what my customers learnt from the post."

How Hollywood Writes A Story

Now that we have listed *your* story topics, let's construct your story.
When a movie keeps your attention for 90 minutes or more, it's because it tells a story in a very specific way.
The story formula is documented in Michael Hague's book *The Hero's 2 Journeys.*
We are going to construct your story in a similar fashion.

I am going to adapt Michael's formula to suit business stories that are generally 1-7 minutes in length.

Your story will be comprised of:

- A **CHARACTER**

  (Hero at the center of the story – That is, you or someone else)

- A **MISSION**

  (A vision or cause that you had that your audience can get behind)

- The **STAKES**

  (Why the mission mattered and what you stood to win/lose. This creates suspense and tension)

- A **ROADBLOCK**

  (The conflict on the path to what you learned and the transformation that resulted. This might be a villain, a challenge, or an enemy. This roadblock generates *emotion*. The bigger the conflict, and the more impossible the challenge, the more engaging the story. Place your time and emphasis here)

- A **TRANSFORMATIONAL RESULT / NEW OPPORTUNITY**

  (The results you got when you overcame the roadblock and how this changed you. This is something that your audience also wants)

What are the Hero's two journeys?

1. The journey of *achievement* – the **results** at the end. For example, you beat the odds and solved a problem. This is probably how you think of most traditional stories –The tale of a journey that leads to a result.
2. The second journey is the journey of *transformation*. The thing that happened within the soul of the main character. It is the unexpected thing learned that changed the main character (hero)'s life for good. This gives the story a **"greater meaning".**

A story leading to a transformation is the key to making people feel good about any movie …
Use this approach in your story and not only will you have more impact on your customers, you will also increase the potential of your customers sticking around and buying more.

TIP : When you tell a story, ask yourself,

"How did the hero of the story change as an individual?"

Here is an example of an "Origin Story", that is, a story of what inspired the formation of a new company or product.

In this case, it is the origin story behind my company and it's my philosophy of helping people in lieu of pitching, in order to sell.

Origin Story Example

(CHARACTER) ...

(I create curiosity by implying that something unexpected happened)

Let me tell you a story about the time when my computer crashed in front of an audience of 100 customers...and how I sold $1M more because of it.

(MISSION)

(I state my mission of renewing a software deal. I create emotion and curiosity by using the word "worried".)

I'd been selling semiconductor software design products for 10 years.

Yet, as I prepared to renew a seven-figure software license deal, I became increasingly worried.

(STAKES)

(I clearly state what we stand to win or lose)

Closing this deal would mean the difference between my product line meeting its sales number for the year or failing to show growth.

... If we failed to show revenue growth, team bonuses would be at stake and the company would question my R&D and marketing budget for next year.

I had plenty of reasons to tell myself that I should be confident.

The customer's business was healthy and their head-count growing.
My goal was to make sure that the competition was kept at bay .... and to attempt to grow revenue during the renewal.

(ROADBLOCK – From Bad to Worse – The low point)

(I lay out the uncertainty of what might happen during the renewal, and then it gets worse, a disastrous computer crash. I amplify the pain that the reader feels by describing exactly how I felt inside.)

I was struggling to gather recent information about this customer's future projects. Without this information about future business opportunities, I couldn't know for sure how this renewal was going to go or truly predict the deal size.

Their management seemed too busy and had been slow to respond when anyone in our account team contacted them. I had heard second-hand that the customer had multiple new projects forming and that this and existing projects were keeping them more than occupied.

I wanted to find out more about what they needed and the new projects they were working on.

So, I decided to hop on a plane and give this customer a "product update, a.k.a. pitch," presentation. I had spent days preparing a pitch that was customized to what I believed to be their needs.

But as I walked on stage to present ...

the unthinkable happened:

My computer crashed right then and there:

The screen, black.

My presentation, gone.

And, stupidly, I hadn't posted it to the cloud or brought a USB stick.

Without even looking, I sensed the peripheral pressure of dozens of eyes in the audience, silently observing my every move.

I felt the blood drain from my body.

Yes, a part of me was desperate, but the stronger side of me was determined not to give up on this renewal ... and on growing revenue.

(TRANSFORMATION)

(The transformation is that this one disaster led to a massive change in how I worked with customers, and this bettered us all.)

I took a deep breath.

In my mind I was talking myself out of the need for presentation slides.

After all, the most charismatic speakers rarely use slides.

What would Tony Robbins or Steve Jobs have done?

Well...

They'd focus on the customer's problem...

And they would probe around to find out about the identity that the customer aspired to.

To them, slides on a screen distracted the audience from what they were saying.

And it was at that point that I decided that I could accomplish my goal without slides.

I began to ask the customer questions (most of which I knew the answers to),

"Tell me about some of the biggest worries that you have right now."

"What's a worst nightmare scenario for you … of what could happen a year from now if you don't find a solution?"

"Why do you think you haven't solved this yet?"

"Where do you want to be two years from now?"

" What would it mean to you personally to succeed?"

and

"How can we help?"

All of a sudden, members of the audience were standing up, writing things down on a whiteboard, explaining exactly what they were working on and their challenges;
telling me all about what excited them about the impact of their projects to society; proud…. of what they had to accomplish.
They explained where they believed there to be a risk – a risk that we could help them avoid.

They were telling me about new projects that they had in store, projects where we could help. (Cha…ching!)

But something even more important had happened here.
I had opened new communication channels and could truly sit back and listen.

Instead of being seen as a salesy person with a PowerPoint pitch, I was now viewed as part of their team.
And they were *convincing themselves* that they

needed our help.

And it was from that day onward that I *"ditched the pitch".*
I stopped pitching and started truly helping my customers using questions and two-way conversations.

We closed an $8M deal … $1M more revenue than our original forecast.

From that point onward, I knew I didn't have to worry about struggling with a renewal… or stand there while customers got bored by my pitch.

(CALL TO ACTION)

(I give the reader a clear and single next step)

My advice?
If you want to serve customers well and draw them closer, ditch the pitch and instead start to help them by using interactive questions and answers – I call this *"Consultative Selling".*
When you sell in this way, customers convince themselves that they need what you are selling.
To find out more about exactly how to do Consultative Selling in your business … Schedule a call here___

YOUR BUSINESS STORY BLUEPRINT

Let's construct your story using the 5 story elements.

CHARACTER

THE LEAD PERSON IN YOUR STORY AND THEIR BACKSTORY
(e.g., You or Your Company's Founder; + Backstory to make people care)

MISSION & VISION

WHY you do what you do, Your PURPOSE, INTENTION, MOTIVE, DESIRE .... and what long-time FEAR or CAUSE led to it
(e.g. Needed a new, lower risk way to get a result; It means a lot to me to help people because that's what people did for me when I was first getting started)

STAKES

WHAT YOU STAND TO WIN OR ARE SCARED WILL HAPPEN IF YOU FAIL ....AND HOW THIS MAKES YOU FEEL?
(Time, Risk, Money, Stress, Struggle, Fear, Doubt, Worry)
(e.g. Shame of losing your job; Fear of not making your sales numbers; Scared to lose money, Risk of delivering product late; Embarrassment of being beaten by a competitor; Frustration of letting customers down).

ROADBLOCK

A CONFLICT, OBSTACLE, ENEMY, VILLAIN. A LOW POINT A THING THAT WENT WRONG. A HARD TO SOLVE PROBLEM
(e.g., Company wouldn't give you any resources; You got fired; Your competition came out with a product that started to eat your lunch)

TRANSFORMATIONAL RESULT

THE NEW OPPORTUNITY & RESULT DISCOVERED
1 key takeaway that you want audience to remember
(e.g., Found a new way to solve a problem and this led to starting your company so that could help others get the same result)

Summary

A few weeks after Steve Jobs had shown his reluctant engineer that, if a MacIntosh Computer could boot up 10 seconds faster, this would save the equivalent of 100 lifetimes per week, the engineer returned *victorious*.
He had shaved 28 seconds off the Mac's start up time.
Jobs succeeded in convincing the engineer by painting a vision.

Whether it is selling or convincing, you too can paint a vision and illustrate an important point using a story.

A business story has five elements,

1. A main character
2. Their mission and vision
3. What's at stake
4. The roadblocks along the path to success, and
5. The transformational result seen

Most people who tell stories omit to talk about roadblocks and what is at stake. Yet these are what keep your audience in suspense and listening

The bigger the roadblock, the more the suspense, and, as in any movie, the more suspense, the more compelling the story.

Most people also forget to talk about the personal toll … and their feelings.
Yet, these feelings of what is going on in your mind are what make the story difficult to ignore.

Keep an inventory of stories as they happen to you during the day.
Note them down during a daily debrief.
Then use them in your communications to keep your audience's attention.

Chapter 7

One Key Takeaway "Make a Lasting Impression"

"Complexity is the enemy of execution."

—Tony Robbins

"Don't fix small problems. Solve big ones."

—Angela Sutton

The Sell Bigger Framework

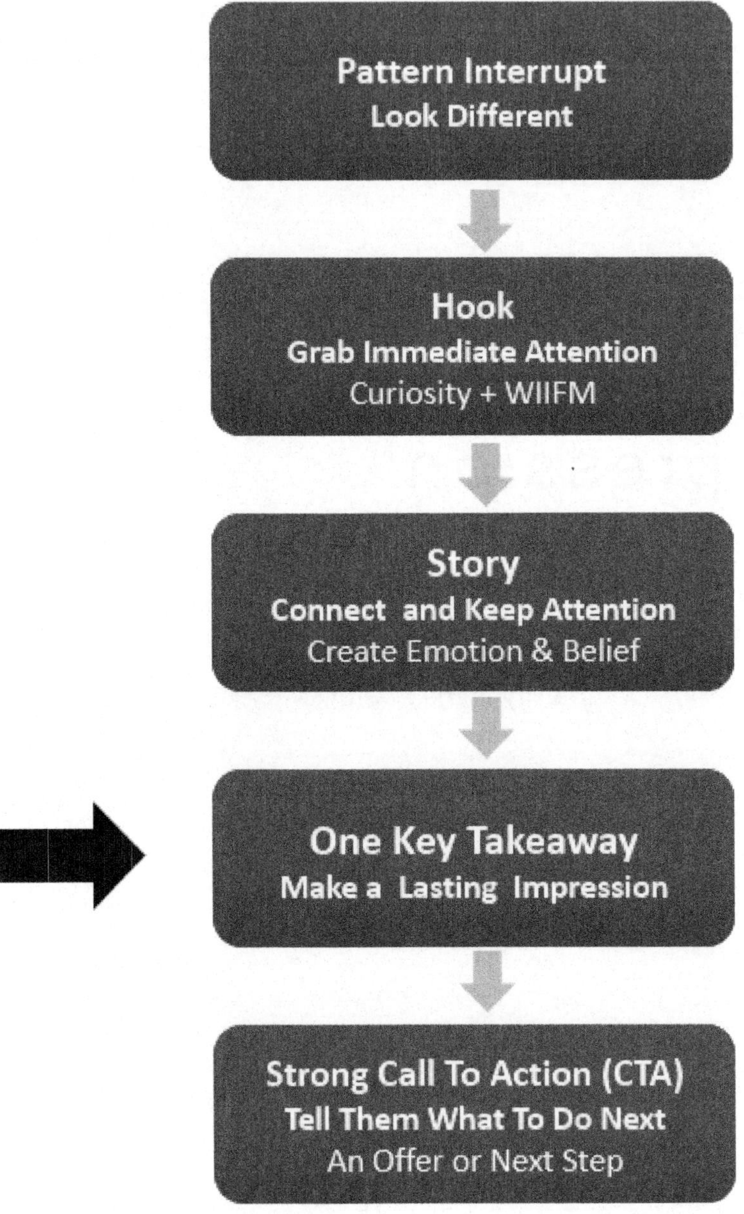

California's Mulholland/Troutdale bridge melted in the Wolsey Fire.

Here is the view that you would have encountered in early 2021 as you approached the bridge.

The question is....
What action should you take if you are driving up to it in a car?

Photo: KC Cooper

The information that answers this question resides on the signs. It is plentiful and fragmented - It caters to every mode of transportation - the bike, the car, the pedestrian.

Yet any one of these people will be guaranteed a struggle as they attempt to figure out what they themselves should do.

When you distill the information on the nine signs, there is one key takeaway, that a single lane remains open and it is to be used by cars only. Others should use a separate pedestrian bridge .

Why do I bring this up? Because long emails catering to a wide audience inevitably become so wound up and complicated that they will fail to get the single most important message across.

The one cupcake of information that each individual needs.

And consider this ....

It is typically 8:30am before I open my email inbox. The first email that I open might be three pages long. It might be titled – *"Comprehensive strategies to improve website layout"* ... Hmmm ...

The topic is right up my street!

That's why I opened the email.

I scan the email quickly, and scroll to the end hoping to find an executive summary in the last paragraph or in the P.S.

I can't find one.

I decide to read the email later, but the reality is, I get busy and I never read it – **The email had one shot at my attention.**

The second email that I open – three sentences – describes one single gem of information about book publishing.
It asks a question that makes me curious.
It answers the question at a high level in the email body with an offer to tell me more if I click on a link. I read the entire email and click.
So, what is wrong with this picture?

The second email contained a single short piece of useful information.
I read the entire email and took action (clicked).

The first email contained much more value.
Yet, I barely consumed it.
And I took no action.

What can we learn?

A *Nature Magazine* research report discusses how people rarely look at a situation that needs improving and decide that the solution is to *remove something* from the current status quo.

(https://www.sciencedaily.com/releases/2021/04/210407135801.htm)

Instead, they default to addition. They add *more detail*, add *more features*, talk about *more benefits*, list an encyclopedia of helpful information.

The truth?

If you want people to remember what you said – make your message *simple* – Have one, and only one, key takeaway.

The point?

When you create your emails, videos and presentations, that you want people to consume, you need to BITE SIZE EACH down to one key takeaway.

Before you write a communication such as a video or email, ask yourself:
"What is the one (and minimal) high impact takeaway that I need to include in order to move the customer to take the next step?"

And
"What is the one big problem that I solve?"

Do this and your communication will have true IMPACT

And drive customers to the next step in the sales process. For example, if my one thing is that I want customers to believe is “My product works”,

Then, my email focuses on a result that a customer got.

“But Angela – What if I have a lot of valuable information to share with a customer? This information gives me credibility!”

I get it.

CHUNK the information up. Turn it into a sequence of short communications that you deliver daily or every couple of days, each one setting up anticipation for the next.
I’ll show you how to do this next.

Chunk Complex Information

If you have volumes of great information at your fingertips, remember your only goal is to convince someone to take the next step.
Your best bet is to CHUNK the information into a series of:

- Messages that each take only 1-2 minutes maximum to read, or
- Videos that each take five minutes or less to consume

Think of this approach as giving your customer just one cupcake at a time.

Six cupcakes in one day would make them feel too full and sick of you.

One cupcake is perfect, leaving them hungry for more.

How do you get people to consume the entire series?

Take a lesson from a TV news show when it breaks for the adverts.

At the end of your first message with your first key takeaway, build demand for the next …like this:

"In my next video/email, I'll show you (2nd takeaway thing that they are curious about).

Look for it tomorrow.

The video/email title will be '____'."

Find Your One Key Takeaway

Your existing presentations, application notes and white papers are full of brilliant takeaways.

Your takeaways usually appear the form of:

- Features
- Benefits
- Advice
- A lesson learned
- Best practices

Let's look at how we can extract the one key takeaway from the myriad of information available.

Let's first step back and look at the real reason that we are communicating with the customer.
It's not to fill the room (or their head) with information that will soon be forgotten.

It is instead to make your customer want to take the next step – To want what you offer.

Suppose that you have a whitepaper or application note that you are using for customer engagement. You want to send out an email or video that prompts people to download it.

The application note or whitepaper might have one top level key takeaway. **One big problem that you solve.**

Or it might have multiple key takeaways.
In which case, we can create a sequence of emails/videos, including one key takeaway in each.

Construct Your One Key Takeaway

The one key takeaway from your communication will usually fall into one of these three categories... An "a-ha" moment; it increases the customer's belief that "it (your product) works", or a "teaching moment". Let's look at each of these.

1. **An "a-ha" moment or Big Idea**

   An a-ha moment causes the customer to have a new realization. For example:

- Why they should have Fear, Uncertainty and Doubt about their current approach or an industry norm, and how to address their fear with your product or method.
  The one key takeaway is that they need to be concerned about a looming problem.

- Something that the customer didn't realize was critical to their business.
  It could be a change looming on the horizon.

  It could be an opportunity to fix a problem that cuts their business risk or saves significant time.
  It could be something that will make them more competitive.

  Suppose you tell your audience your company's origin story. The story outlines a new opportunity or way to address a problem.
  The one key takeaway is ....

  How your solution or method solves the audience's specific problem and how it will make them *feel*.
  It talks about what you were feeling and thinking at the very moment when you created it or discovered the solution that you now offer them.

A Big Idea takes this a step further – It causes the customer to have a new vision about how things could be if they buy from you

2. "It works"

Your communication simply reinforces with evidence that the customer can get a desired result. This is the one key takeaway.

The communication includes supporting information. Your communication might be a demo, customer story, quote or testimonial.

- The one key takeaway is that your solution gives a customer the result that they too want, and how it will make them feel.

ACTION SHEET:

Construct One Key Takeaway To Insert Into Your Email, Video, Or Presentation

---

A-HA MOMENT

Why they should feel fear, uncertainty, doubt

Something that they didn't realize

New Opportunity to fix a problem

HOW IT MAKES A CUSTOMER FEEL:

IT WORKS

Customer Testimonial
Customer Quote
Customer Story
Demo

HOW IT MAKES A CUSTOMER FEEL:

3. A Teaching Moment

In a teaching moment, your key takeaway, describes a FEATURE of your product that can produce a specific RESULT.

But you don't stop at that...
This is what most people miss:

You will want to describe how the *result* fulfills a customer's *DESIRES*.

You might well be used to framing this kind of information in this traditional way:

"features + benefits"

Instead of features and benefits, we will use a more compelling approach that connects the benefit to its result, and then to the customer's emotional desires.

Your one key takeaway will talk about:

"Feature – Result – Desires"

The desires will sell the result, *emotionally*
The desire may talk about what the result meant to the customer personally – that he or she felt more happy and encountered less stress.

Why does this approach work?

Customers buy in order to get *results*.

And they also buy because of internal *desire* to feel better – For example they want to get rid of recurring pain.

Construct FEATURE – RESULT – DESIRES (One Key Takeaway)

Select the one feature that you want to talk about in your communication

Use the following statement to construct a Feature, its Result and the Desire statement :

> My Product or Offer
>
> Has (FEATURE)
>
> **Which helps you to get** _____ (RESULT)
>
> (Or ... so that you can get ______ (RESULT)
>
> (Or ... so that you don't have to do ____ (PAINFUL THING)
>
> **Which means you can** _____ (DESIRE)

How should you describe the *result* and the *desire*?

How To Describe The Customer's Result

The *result* is the thing that the customer wants to get when they buy your product or offer.

Why? Because the *result* helps the customer to be more competitive, with less risk, in less time.

Examples of the result include: "My product ...

- Automates these manual tasks ____ ."

- Saves you this much money ___."
- Finishes the job in 25% less time."
- Gets the job done predictably with less worry."
- Increases your profit."
- Maintains 99.9% uptime."

So, what is the desire that this result fulfils?

How To Describe The Customer's Desire

The *Desire* is what your customer *feels*, personally and professionally, after they buy.

It will be one or more of these six things:

1. RELIEF FROM PAIN so that the customer feels less stressed
2. Increases STATUS or re-enforces an IDENTITY that the customer wants. This identity or status makes the customer feel good about themselves. For example, with your product, they can now think of themselves as cool, sophisticated, successful or part of a group of like-minded, visionary people.
3. The joy of a SPECIALIZED / SPECIFIC solution that delivers the security of a tailored fix for their exact problem.
4. A GREAT EXPERIENCE delivered during and after a purchase, so that the customer feels like they matter to you and thinks of you favorably.
5. Gain a NEW OPPORTUNITY to fix a problem in a way that is unique. The customer feels excited, leading edge and smart .... and can now jump ahead of their competition.

6. A BIGGER REASON - .... such that the customer feels spiritually enriched. The reason may involve the customer helping their community, family, or improving their own personal health/wealth/relationships. That reason might also deliver the customer more freedom, Examples of bigger reason include:

- "You can enjoy more time with your family."
- "You will no longer worry about meeting payroll."
- "You feel secure with the knowledge that someone has your back."
- "Your boss will appreciate you."
- "You will be admired by your peers."
- "You can kiss goodbye to long weekends at the office."

Constructing Your Feature-Result-Desires

Let's construct a single Feature-Result-Desires trio to insert into an email, video or presentation. Here's an example

FEATURE NAME:

7-STEP Email writing system

RESULT:

So that you can ___
Or ... So that you can avoid ___
Or ... Which helps you to ___

Get customer's attention so that they stop thinking of you as an annoying salesperson and instead will be both happy to hear from you and eager to respond

DESIRE:

Which means that ...

(STATUS) You will meet and beat your sales quota long before quarter end.
No more looking stupid when your boss asks what's new in a major sales account
(SPECIALIZED) You can deliver customers the tailored help that they desperately need and make them want to buy more
(GREAT EXPERIENCE) You will feel proud that you delivered the best possible customer service
(PAIN RELIEF/BIGGER REASON)
You will not miss your daughter's soccer game because you felt pressured to stay late at the office

Desires are:

1. PAIN RELIEF
2. STATUS / IDENTITY
3. SPECIALIZED / SPECIFIC
4. GREAT EXPERIENCE
5. NEW OPPORTUNITY
6. A BIGGER REASON

ACTION SHEET: Feature-Result-Desires

Construct your own single Feature-Result-Desire to insert into your email, video or presentation

FEATURE NAME:

RESULT:

So you can ___
Or ... So you can avoid ___
Or ... Which helps you to ___

DESIRE:

Which means that ...

Desires are:

1. **PAIN RELIEF**
2. **STATUS / IDENTITY**
3. **SPECIALIZED / SPECIFIC**
4. **GREAT EXPERIENCE**
5. **NEW OPPORTUNITY**
6. **A BIGGER REASON**

Summary

Being brief is difficult.

But it plays a vital role in effective customer communication. Your customers are rarely going to read a three-page email or listen with full attention to a one-hour presentation about your product's features and benefits.
To ask them to do so is to simply overwhelm them, setting them up to forget what you said.

Your message will get lost. So what to do:

Narrow each communication down to one key takeaway.
Create sequences of multiple, separate bite-sized chunks of communications if what you have to say is complex
For example create a sequence of daily emails, each with one key takeaway

The good news?

Customers are happy to give an email containing a couple of sentences a gander, especially if there is a P.S. at the bottom of the email or a summary that articulates the essence of your message and what to do next.

If you are considering making a video that is longer than five minutes, consider chunking it into multiple videos, each less than five minutes long.

The point?

Have one key takeaway – the one thing that you want the audience to do or remember – in every communication that you create.

Your one key takeaway might be an "a-ha" moment or "big idea", a case study or demo of your product that proves that "it works".
Or your one key takeaway may be a teaching moment; For example, how to use a particular *feature*.

Remember that the customer doesn't care so much about features. The customer cares about *results*.

They will want your product if it has a feature that fulfills either a personal or professional *desire* that makes their lives easier, more spiritually fulfilled and less full of fear.

For this reason, a feature-based key takeaway should include the desire that the feature meets as well as the results that it generates.

Chapter 8

The Call To Action/Offer "Tell Them What To Do Next"

"The greatest leader is not necessarily the one who does the greatest things.
He is the one that gets the people to do the greatest things."

—Ronald Reagan

"A confused buyer always says 'no'."

—Stephen Larson

The Sell Bigger Framework

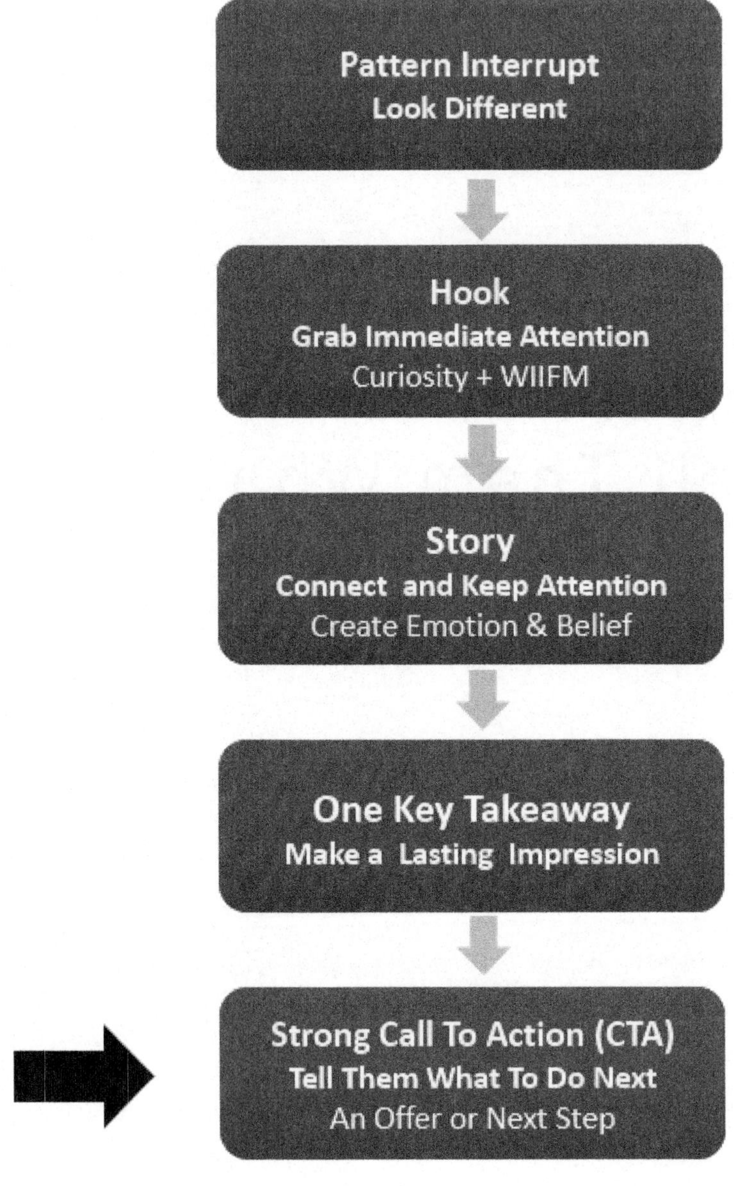

In Daniel Kahneman's book, *Thinking Fast, and Slow*, he talks about why people react like they do ...

He cites an example of how the mind responds in two parts when viewing a picture of an angry lady's face.

- Part #1 of the mind's response is an **automatic** and quick reaction.
  This reaction requires next to no effort, and little thinking.
- Part #2 of the mind's response is more **intentional** and calculated. The mind analyzes the situation before deciding what to do.

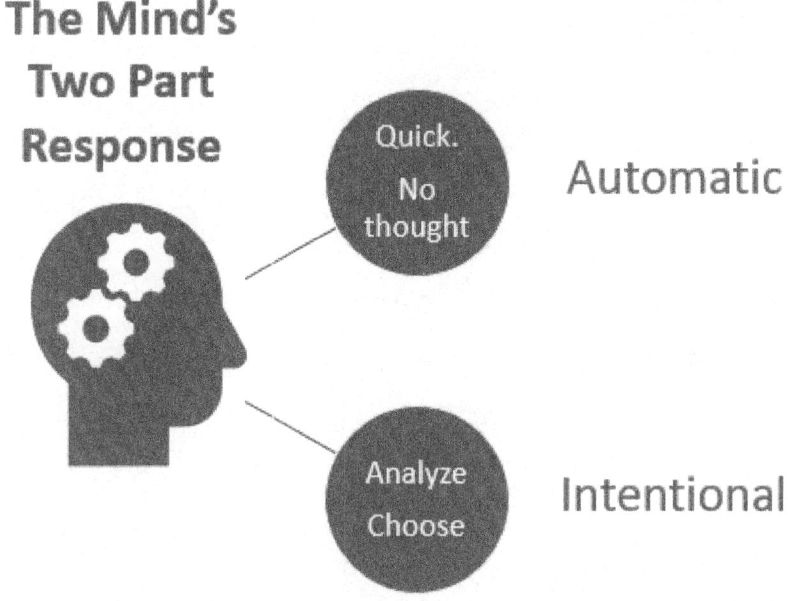

Why do I raise this?

Because the **purpose of sending your communication to a customer is to get them to take action**; to take a next step.

You see, the biggest mistake that people make in white papers, emails, and presentations is that they don't ask the customer to take *action*.

So how do you make your communication actionable?

You cater both to the Automatic and Intentional response systems of the brain.

Types Of Call To Action

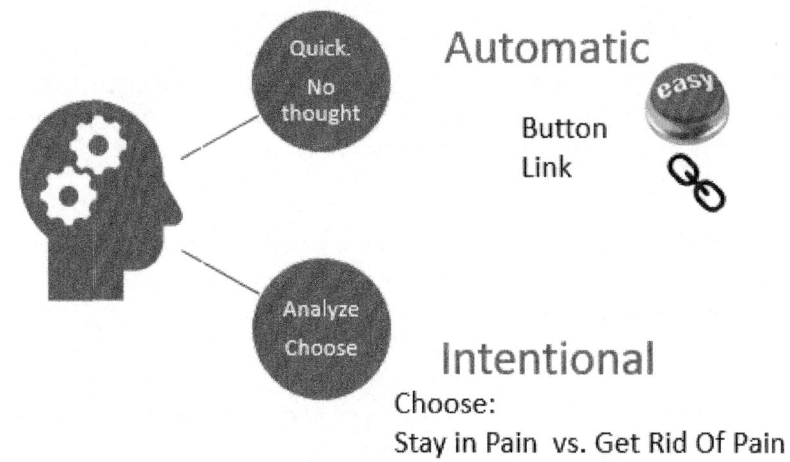

In order to make a sale, we have all been told that:

"You need to ask the customer for the sale."

Any communication with the customer is similar... We should *"Ask the customer to take a next step "* – with A CALL TO ACTION

Which leads to my point:

A communication needs to include either an AUTOMATIC or INTENTIONAL action for the customer to take. That is it needs

An obvious "EASY BUTTON" or LINK to appeal to the brain's willingness to take AUTOMATIC action:
For example: "Click here"

A clearly articulated choice between "get out of pain" or "stay in pain"... This appeals to the brain's INTENTIONAL

ACTION.

For example:
"Yes, sign me up to try your software for 14 days FREE" vs.
"No – I prefer to keep getting poor performance doing this___ manually."

Conclude every communication with a *strong* call to action (CTA) such as a "Click Here" link or button.

TIP: In general, only have one call to action that you ask a customer to perform next (and multiple links to that same action within your communication).

Here are some examples of a CTA that you might include in an email:

- P.S. Hit reply if you would like me to send you the presentation slides.
- Click here to download the scripts for free.
- Grab your FREE cheat sheets here.
- Click here to find out how CUSTOMER achieved RESULT.
- What's your biggest problem in achieving your goal? Let me know and I'll address it in my next Facebook Live Q&A session.

  Note: This is a powerful example of an open-ended question to engage an audience and to find out what interests them.
- Go here to download the five FREE templates.
- Comment below this post if you would like to attend the free Masterclass.
- Invest by May 31st and receive a free upgrade plus three free bonuses and templates that show you exactly how to complete your first design in less than a week.

Where To Place The CTA Within Your Communications

You will want to place the CTA in any communication in a place where the customer will look for it first. Specifically, put the CTA in these places:

1. Email:
    a. In the P.S.
    b. Optionally, include the same CTA right below the headline
    c. If your email includes a link to play a video, or call to action, have the thumbnail picture of the video "above the fold" with a "play" button superimposed on it.
    d. Include a single call to action such as "watch this video", or "download this whitepaper" in your generic email footer that you use for all emails that you send out every day.
2. White paper/article:
    a. In your conclusion, introduction and bio.

        "Go here to get this FREE download ____"

        or

        "For more information, go here ____"
3. Video
    a. Below the video (have a button to click on). Tell customers to click on it during the video
4. Web pages:
    a. Prominently, near the top of the page. (don't require the viewer have scroll to find the CTA)

Using Buttons For Your Call To Action

Any button tempts the mind's automatic response #1.

Its very presence invokes *curiosity.*

How do you increase the chance that the button will create an automatic response and be pressed?

- Make your button BIG
- Give your button a distinct color
- State on the CTA button itself the BENEFIT or RESULT the audience will get if they press. For example:

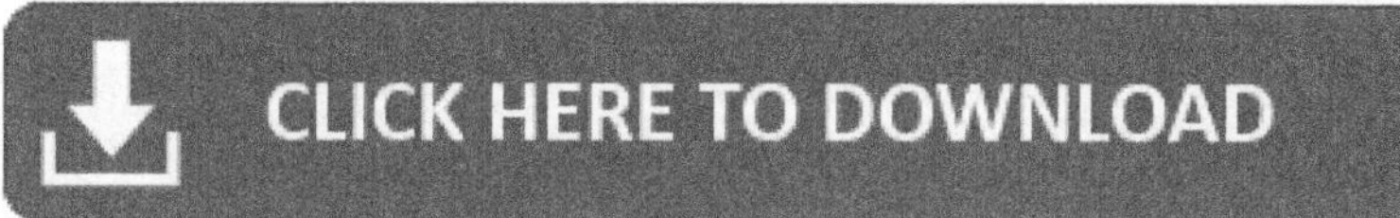

How can you make the button appeal to the brain's *intentional* reaction?

Preface the button with a reason to act now; a deadline, a consequence of inaction.

Something that makes the view have to choose.

For example:

"This offer expires at midnight on October 23rd."

Let's now take a look at some specific call to action buttons

CTA Buttons

Here is the format of the wording that appears on the button"

Button Format 1: "ICON , (ACTION) (IMMEDIATE BENEFIT)" Or "(ACTION) (IMMEDIATE BENEFIT) ICON"

Examples:

CLICK HERE TO SAVE YOUR FREE SPOT NOW 

Button Format 2: " (ICON) Yes, GIVE ME (BENEFIT)"

Examples:

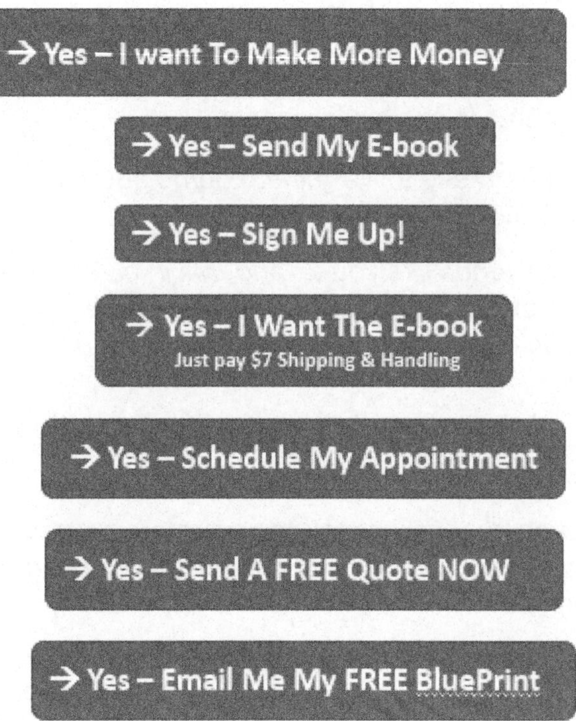

Written Text Call To Action

Buttons are very appealing… But what if you want to just use text (and a link) as a CTA?

Here's what to do

> **Text Link Format**
> "Do THIS (by DEADLINE) to get (BENEFIT)"
>
> "Do THIS (by DEADLINE) to TAKE NEXT STEP"

Examples for emails or presentations:

- *"Go here to see a five-minute demo about how (CUSTOMER) solved (PROBLEM)"*
- *"If this sounds like you … and this interests you, someone technical will be happy to chat and answer your specific questions. Just click here to set up a call this week."*
- *"Click here to let me know what your biggest design concerns are."*
- *"Hop on over and check this page out right now to find out how you can get (RESULT) without changing your design flow."*
- *"BTW, if you are busy right now with a deadline, pop an appointment in my online calendar here so we can chat once your deadline has passed."*

  "Change the appointment at any time. We'll make it happen."
- *"Watch the video here by Wednesday, after which we will be taking it down permanently."*

Example for social media posts:

- *"Comment below to tell me what your biggest roadblocks are."*

- *"View the video here."*
- *"Look here for more free examples.*

The Email P.S.

Later in this book, I will talk about how to have a lasting impact with "skip readers".

But, for now, know that **an Email P.S. is a must in *every* email to a customer.**

An Email P.S. is where the email "skip reader's" or over-whelmed executive's eyes gravitate to ...

The P.S. is your parting shot in any communication.

In the P.S., reiterate
... the RESULT and BENEFIT that your offer will generate
... and the CTA itself.

TIP: Preface the P.S. With a statement that implies it is an *afterthought*, just like Lt. Columbo used to do in the TV hit series.

Afterthought format

"Oh, before I forget ..."

"Oh, one more thing ...."

"Hey, did you know? ...."

"Hey, BTW ...."

P.S. Format:
AFTERTHOUGHT: "Do THIS (by DEADLINE) to get (RESULT)"

"AFTERTHOUGHT: "Do THIS (by DEADLINE) to (TAKE NEXT STEP)"

Examples:

- *"P.S. Hey, BTW, did you know that (doing this) helps (pick one of: save money, make money, save time, avoid effort)*
  Click on the link below to download the free PDF that shows you how to (save money, make money, save time, avoid effort, eat your competition's lunch)."
- *"P.S. Hey, BTW… Click on the link to book a free call and find out more. Change your appointment at any time."*
- *"P.S. Oh, one more thing …. Tomorrow I will send you an email which answers this in detail. Be sure to check it out." The email title will be (TITLE)"*
- *"P.S Hey – Did you know that, for the next week, you can get my complete set of templates for free by clicking here?"*

The Email Footer

You send emails all day. Every single one sent outside of the company is a free advertising opportunity !

Always add to your email footer template *one* link to engage the customer.

Email Footer Format: "DO THIS to get (BENEFIT/RESULT) "

Email Footer Examples:

- *"Sign Up For Our May 2-4, 2021, User Conference before April 22nd."*

- *"Find out how to get (RESULT). Download the white paper here."*
- *"Find out how to get (BENEFIT) for your specific situation. Schedule a call with me in my calendar here."*
- *"Sign up to receive weekly (BENEFIT) tips, delivered directly to your mailbox every Monday. Over 1000 people have already signed up."*
- *"Join our exclusive private Facebook Community here for free to get tips on how to get (RESULT) ."*

What To Do If Your CTA Is "WATCH THIS VIDEO"

What if the CTA of your email, or webpage is to "watch a video"?
How can you tempt your customer to click to watch the video?

The best way to tempt the brain's "automatic response" is to present a thumbnail with a "play button".
Incent a click by including in your email or webpage what looks like a video thumbnail – that is, a picture of the video with a "play" button on top.

Pressing on the thumbnail will take your audience to the video playback.

Here's how to create the thumbnail:

Create A Video Thumbnail (to use in an email or webpage)

What to do if your CTA is "WATCH THIS VIDEO"

What if your CTA in an email, online presentation or webpage is to "**watch a video**"? How can you tempt your customer to click and watch?

Include a video thumbnail with a play button on it using the following steps. Pressing on the thumbnail will take your audience to the video playback. Here's how to create the thumbnail

1. Take snapshot picture of video (Use SNAGIT or SNIP & SKETCH TOOL)

2. Find a play button graphic using Google search "Play button PNG"

3. Combine the play button graphic and snapshot in an editor e.g., PowerPoint and save result as JPG (or snapshot it again)

4. Include thumbnail in your communication and link it to video so that when people click on the thumbnail it will take them to the actual video

Link thumbnail to video playback, for example, on YouTube

TIP: Add a text link to the video underneath the thumbnail, in case the customer has problems viewing thumbnail images

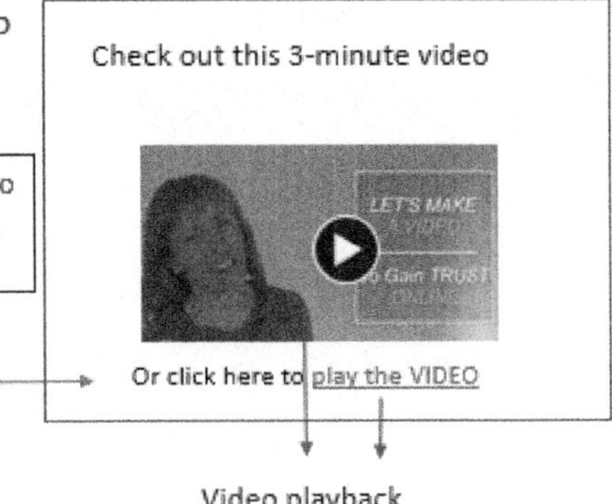

The Offer (OPTIONAL)

If you plan to "ask for the sale" in your communication, present it in the form of an *offer*.

An offer is more than just your product and its price. Your offer slides should additionally include:

- **YOUR PRODUCT** (e.g. your software)
- **OBJECTION REMOVERS:** Items that will specifically **remove excuses and objections** (e.g., training and migration tools that remove learning curve worries)
- **RESULTS CREATORS: Additional items that increase the customer's confidence in their ability to get results** (e.g. swipe files, onboarding, free training)
- **URGENCY: Reason to act now** (e.g., bonus material)

Your OFFER =

Your Product

+

Results creators

(Accelerators and tools that make the customer feel confident that they will get results)

+

Urgency creators

(Reasons to act now)

+

Objection removers

(Accelerators/tools/services that remove their objections)

Here's an example of an offer.

Example OFFER

12 months' software access

50 training modules

24/7 customer support

Working Case Studies and examples you can swipe and then modify, so that you can get up to speed in no time

Migration tool that imports your design from (COMPETITOR'S SOFTWARE) and verifies the result

If you buy before January 22nd

Free tickets to our virtual user conference on Feb 26th

Concierge service to get your first design finished.

3-pay payment plan available

Summary

A big mistake that people make when communicating with customers is that they fail to suggest “the next step”.

Always include a *single* call to action (CTA) in any communication, to prompt a clear and easy response from your customers.

As Daniel Kahneman in his book, *Thinking Fast, and Slow,* is quick to point out, viewers have two reactions when they read or see a communication from you:

- An *automatic* and quick response. This requires little to no effort or thinking.
- An *intentional*, calculated response, where customers analyze and deliberately choose what to do next

A viewer’s *automatic* response can be prompted by a tempting button, video thumbnail with playback button or a link, where the link/button states the benefit of pressing it promptly.

Make your CTA stick out like a sore thumb in the place that the viewer will surely look.

- Repeat the CTA in your email’s P.S.
- Make the CTA the first thing someone sees when they view a webpage.
- If your CTA is to ask someone to play a video, use a video thumbnail with a tempting “play” button superimposed on it. Pressing on the thumbnail takes the viewer to a webpage that will play back the video.

The *intentional* part of the viewer’s response can be prompted by giving the viewer a reason to act; a deadline, clear benefit, or stated consequences if they don’t act. Include this in the P.S. of your email or in a prominent place.

Chapter 9

What To Say

"Seek First To Understand, Then To Be Understood"

—Stephen Covey—from the book *"7 Habits Of Highly Effective People"*

I was 13, and sitting in a physics class at school, mesmerized. My interest in physics and chemistry had been piqued from an early age by my amazing dad who was a brilliant chemical engineer by trade.

Physics and chemistry were now *my* passion, too!

These subjects just clicked for me.

I was fascinated by how they explained and predicted the way that things around me operated.

From why braking a car made the brake pads turn hot, to why it took so much effort to "get started" when I rode my bike, yet moving along was easy once I got going;

why a stream of water from a tap was attracted to a comb after I combed my hair with it.

And why, when you spray something out of an aerosol can, the whole can turns ice cold.

These classes formed the foundation of everything that I do today.

So, as I opened up my end-of-term school report, my heart sank when I set eyes on this somber comment from my Physics teacher,
"Angela is rather quiet. She needs to learn to ask more questions in class instead of taking a back seat."

Say what ?

That single comment changed my life.

I am so grateful to my teacher, Dr. Hands, for speaking up on that day.

He instantly turned me into the person that I am now, "the one who always asks questions."

I didn't care whether or not asking questions made me look stupid. The conversations that ensued when I did so were amazing. And my classmates would furiously scribble down the answers given ... telling me that my questions helped all. And I felt such unity with them because of this.

Oftentimes, my question was about something they had not thought about – A detail that ended up deepening everyone's understanding.

Sometimes, I was just seeking to confirm that I understood what was being taught; gain clarity, and temper misconceptions before they snowballed.

My point?

Asking a question is the single best way to improve your communication channel with a customer.

- To ask your customer to help you help them.
- To ask for confirmation and clarity so that you can avoid errors or a misunderstanding with your customer
- To reassure the customer you are *actually listening*.

And, since the topic of this chapter is "What to Say", let's flip this observation around.

- What questions do customers ask *you*? ... and why?
- What can you learn from these questions about how you can better serve your customers... so that you can sell more?
- How will your customers know that you care?
- What knowledge do your customers not yet realize that they need to have, that will help them?

We will use questions as our guide to generate topics to write about in the Action Sheet at the end of this chapter.

What you can talk about in any communication will generally fall into three categories:

- How to solve a problem
- A "Big Idea"
- Connection

Let's discuss each.

How To

"How To" Communications answer a frequently asked question by showing the customer **"how to"** do something or solve a problem.
The customer will gain a quick success.
Topic examples:
"How to solve (PROBLEM)"
"5 ways to reduce (PROBLEM)"

A "Big Idea"

A **"big idea"** communication delivers a new perspective on how to solve a problem or think about a problem

You can do this at the macro level by painting a *vision* of where your company is headed and why it matters to the company and you – Your "Why?"

You can portray a "big idea" with respect to a product that you sell too. How?
Change the way a customer thinks about solving a problem.
How specifically?
First, make the customer *self-identify* with a big problem that they have by describing its symptoms to them quantitatively.
Topic: *"Is this you? You do (this) 5 times a week to solve (problem) and yet you feel ___ and are unsure about _____"?*
Your goal is to get the customer thinking "Yes--- That's me!"
Next, counter their old belief that what they have is the best solution and replace it with a *new belief* that you offer something superior.

Show how you solve the problem differently and that this presents a new *opportunity* to them.
Then give them a choice on whether they want to keep their old belief or chose to fix the problem with your product.

This type of communication is very effective in removing sales objections
Topic examples:

> *"Most people think__, when the truth is___"*
> *"Doing (old way) is costing you money."*
> *"A vs. B… Which is better?"*

Connection

A **connection** communication messages: "Why I care".

This communication will be full of empathy and how you feel. It will talk about shared experiences -- how you have been where the customer is now or what happened to you in a similar situation to theirs.
It will talk about how it felt when you were in their situation and why this very experience inspires you every day to help customers like them.

The customer will then believe that you understand them and care.
As a result, they think of you as a kindred spirit, a friend that they can trust.

You can also connect with customers via customer testimonials and other proof that your product does exactly what they want.

> Topic examples:
>
> *"The time when I had (similar problem to you)"*
>
> *"You became a (JOB TITLE) because you care about ___"*

"What it meant to (CUSTOMER) to solve (PROBLEM), once and for all"

Three Categories of Communication

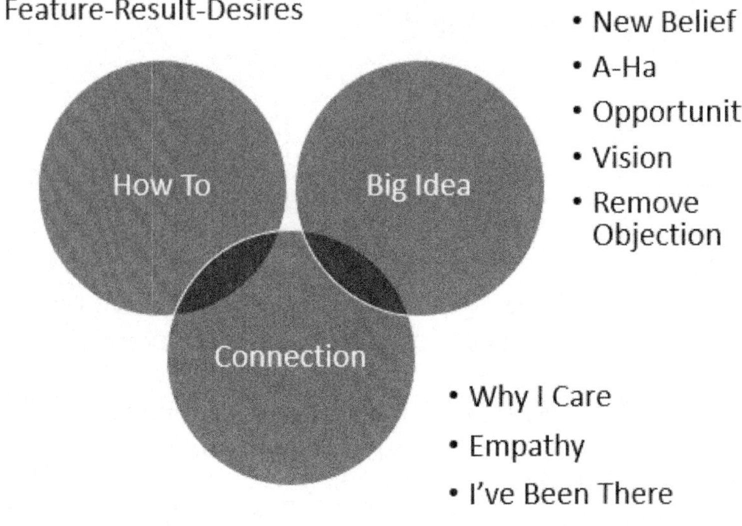

Fill out the following Action Sheet with possible topics to write about.

ACTION SHEET: Topics To Write About

Not sure what topics to write about? Fill out this action sheet.

1. **"HOW TO". A Specific PROBLEM and Its SOLUTION/Tip and what it will mean to them**

   A Quick Success, FAQ

2. **"BIG IDEA"**

   Misconceptions In The Market Place. Opportunities, Vision Objection removal.

   "Most people think__, when the truth is___"

   "A vs. B... Which is better?"

3. **CONNECTION - WHY I CARE - Empathy.**

   How it makes me feel to help you

   "I've been where you are"

   Testimonials

Summary

To this day, I am the first to raise my hand with a question.

And you must not hold back when it comes to asking questions of your customers.

Because that is how you can better serve them and sell them more.

You should make a note of the questions that they ask during your conversations with them, or that they ask customer support.
Use these as inspiration for what you communicate;
As "excuses" to contact them with open arms.

Their answers will tell you what topics to write about, and these typically fall into 3 categories:

- **"How To". A problem and a tip or solution** to help your customer gain a quick success. Talk about examples and what this solution will mean to them, personally and professionally
- **A "big idea"** – Your "Why", often driven by a misconception in the marketplace or something that changed your perspective. Educate the customer on the true answer. Share your vision.
  In doing so, create new beliefs about what's possible
- **Connection: "Why I care"** and have empathy for my customer's situation – A personal story that relates to your customer that shows them why it is meaningful to you to help them. How you have been where they are today. People buy from folks that they believe care about them.

Cover all 3 categories as you communicate with customers. Mix it up! And you will develop a close bond with your customer.

PART 3

Putting It To Work In Your Business

"If you focus on service, money chases you."

—Prince EA

*"When you hear something, you forget it.
When you see something, you remember it.
But not until you actually do something will you understand it."*

—Chinese Proverb

A communication, a book, is of little use if you read it, yet don't apply it.

In this section you will apply the Sell Bigger Framework directly to your emails, presentations, webinars, masterclasses, voicemails, whitepapers, journals and articles, webpages and videos.

By modeling the examples and by using the action sheets provided.

The purpose of sending out your communication is to get your customer to *pay attention* and to *respond in one very specific way*—with one specific next step (call to action) and to leave the customer with *one specific feeling that you care*

Let's get started.

Chapter 10

Fix Your Broken Emails

"Marketing is not about generating lots of content. It's about having that content drive a customer to the next step."

—Angela Sutton

"I don't have a budget or a project starting right now, but your email caught my eye, and made me think.

I wanted to thank you for that and let you know that, when we are starting a new project, I will be contacting you."

I love receiving emails like the above.

Not only does it make me grin that someone enjoyed my email.

But it also means that we just started a new conversation. I am standing out from the pack!

In this day and age, it's often considered a miracle if a customer opens your email, let alone responds.

So how exactly can we make our emails stand out?

We do this using the "Sell Bigger Framework".

It starts with the creation of a great headline that compels the reader to open the email...

Then a great story to keep their interest and make a lasting impression

This is followed by a key takeaway that enlightens the customer.

Finally a call to action that guides the customer to the next step.

In this chapter, you will see eight everyday examples of emails that take the steps above in order to drive sales.

How To Use The "Sell Bigger" Framework

To create emails that people open and take action on, we're going to use the "Sell Bigger" Framework format. That is:

Pattern Interrupt – Hook – Story – One Key Takeaway – Call To Action

We will look at eight complete email examples designed to engage the customer. These emails will help you to retain customers and grow business in existing sales accounts.

These emails, for the most part, may also be used for lead generation that drives brand new business.

The 8 examples will:

- Invite a customer to a face-to-face or private teleconference meeting
- Invite a customer to a webinar, masterclass broadcast, or event
- Spotlight a feature or a new software product release
- A "big idea". Change a customer's way of thinking in order to create interest/curiosity ...or to remove a common objection before the customer even asks....
- Revive a customer relationship or show a customer that you truly care... by connecting with them on a personal level after you haven't spoken for a while
- Offer a Free giveaway to help your customer – For example, online training, onboarding, a whitepaper - in order to create goodwill and start a new conversation
- Show a customer "how to" do something
- Ask what your customer is doing, so you can help, and drive additional sales

As we analyze the content and structure of these emails, you will see how you can build something similar for your own customers.

Here is the email structure that we will use.

PATTERN INTERRUPT (optional)	😎 **Subject Line Prefix that is an Emoji.** **Powerful word. Word in brackets such as** *[PDF]* or a quantified number embedded within the subject line such as *"#1" or 47"*
HOOK	<u>**Your email's main subject line**</u> The headline includes **CURIOSITY and WIIFM** to tempt your audience to open the email
STORY	The main body of the message **Pictures/text that tell a story leading into the one key takeaway that you want your customer to remember**
ONE KEY TAKEAWAY	A big idea or an answer to one big problem or misconception that they have • **Keep it brief**– save detail for the PDF or video that you are offering in the NEXT STEP • **Talk about RESULTS and what it will MEAN to your customer personally to fix the problem** *"We solved this for ___ by following five simple steps .... And this meant that we could ___"*
CTA, OFFER	The one very specific thing that you want the customer to do next. e.g., DO THIS by (DEADLINE) to get (BENEFIT) For example: *"CLICK HERE before Jan 15 to get the free PDF"*
	Regards, *YOURNAME*
CTA, OFFER *repeated*	P.S. **Reiterate CTA/OFFER and deadline** because the P.S. is where skip reader will look !

Let's take a look at the eight examples:

1. Invite To A Face To Face Meeting or Private Teleconference Call/Webinar

"One on one" calls and webinars can be a powerful sales tool. Yet how do you get your customer to agree to grant you their precious time for such a meeting?

In this email example, I immediately grab the customer's attention by alluding to a familiar movie – Groundhog Day – I am using a technique known as a "Key Point Story" , covered in more detail in my story-telling training course.

But you can get the idea from the example. I recount a short story about a familiar topic and then relate it to the problem that my meeting or webinar will help the customer address.

Specifically, I relate how Groundhog Day recurs in the movie, again and again, to the customer's end of quarter sales scramble.
Something that recurs every quarter with no good solution in sight.

The rather unconventional title of "⏰ **What standing still in time and a ground squirrel can teach you about sales."**

certainly makes my email stand out, as does the clock emoji. The title exudes massive curiosity, making it highly likely that my email will get opened.

HOOK ⏰**What standing still in time and a ground squirrel can teach you about sales.**

STORY In the movie, *Groundhog Day,* Bill Murray plays the part of Phil Connors, a TV Weatherman covering the Groundhog Day event in Punxsutawney, Pennsylvania.

He gets forced to relive February 2nd, Groundhog Day, again and again.

Once he realizes that the day repeats itself, he experiments with using this to his advantage ... but becomes frustrated with the repetition; reliving the day again and again with no escape in sight.

Only after he transforms himself into a good, considerate person does he wake up to find that it is February 3rd

One Key Takeaway So why do I raise this?
Because, if you are like I was, **you are busy chasing perfection and near-term goals on your own, and you sometimes push the customer so hard, feeling that you are going around and around in circles to close sales at quarter end....** It frustrates you. EVERY quarter end, repetition - and the same story.
– It feels like the ritual of the quarter end sales crunch will never end.

And all of this when what you really would like is a new approach that makes you feel good. I am talking about making sure that customers perceive you as a person who cares, first and foremost, while you are still closing sales.

What if you could approach customers the

***right* way the *first* time so that they were receptive to your sales offer throughout the quarter?**

So that they actually *return your phone calls*?

And what if you **felt good,** instead of pushy when you try to upsell your customer?

CTA If you are an **ambitious sales professional who wants to end the quarter-end scramble ... and have customers respond to your emails and voicemails throughout the quarter, please join me for this complementary 30-minute masterclass.**

I will run it live on **Thursday, June 21st at 10am Pacific time.**

I will show you what to say and **the five triggers you can use to get customers to respond;** triggers that work because they show the customer that you care.

To your success,
YOURNAME

P.S. **Sign up here for the complementary 30-minute masterclass where you will learn how to get customers to respond to your emails and voicemails, every day of the sales quarter, so as to minimize the quarter end sales crunch.**

2. Invitation To A Webinar/ Masterclass Broadcast

When you send out an invitation to a webinar or masterclass, folks might be tempted to sign up ... or not.

How do you make your invitation so compelling that they have a hard time resisting?

And, once you have got them to register, how do you make enough of a lasting impression to make them want to actually show up?

By telling the STORY behind the content of that webinar or masterclass. Why it means something to you? What inspired it? And the results that you want them to see.

The customer feels compelled to sign up when they can see what's in it for them

Yet, they also feel compelled to sign up when they now know that you are simply trying to share the benefit of what you and your customers have learnt in the past.

The email's story shifts the customer's perception away from the dread of being pitched to the joy of being helped. It's a story of transformation.

Transformation: Being pitched → Being helped

Stories will motivate people to show up.

This webinar invitation email example will be familiar to you. It is my personal story of transformation – That led to the founding of my Company.

HOOK **TITLE: How My Lousy Presentation to 100 Customers Grew The Deal Size By $1M**

STORY A dark, blank screen. My laptop – Dead.

It happened just 10 seconds after I jumped on stage in front of a room of about 100 people who worked for my largest customer.

A $7M software renewal was at stake and my perfect presentation, carefully crafted, designed to show my customer what we had on the horizon for them, had just evaporated.

I instantly felt cold beads of sweat around my neck.
I became painfully aware that my face was turning red.

What should I do?

Out of desperation, I began a conversation with the audience.
Asked them questions that I already knew the answers to about their design projects and what changes I thought they might want to see in our software to support this.

I wrote their answers on the white board.

To my surprise, the audience suddenly began chipping in advice.
They were eagerly paying attention.

We were having a conversation instead of me lecturing them.

They were asking clarifying questions. And they were telling me about new projects that they were planning that we could help them with.

The result? **They felt like they had been heard; that I wasn't just some suit there to pitch**

them – painting exaggerated pictures of how wonderful our product was.

We **uncovered new sales opportunities** during that conversation as we talked deeply about what they were trying to do with our software.

One Key Takeaway The result? The renewal revenue was $1M larger than we had expected ...

.... and I had the pleasure of meeting a **room full of engaged customers instead of bored ones.**

It was from that point onward that **I stopped pitching**

and instead made my presentations interactive – a conversation!
In doing so, my customers felt invested in the solution that we were delivering, and keen to buy more.

They felt like we were listening to them and cared.
So let me ask you this.

How would it feel if you spent less time preparing the perfect presentation.... And instead spent your time asking your customers the right questions;
questions that let **customers *convince themselves* that they needed what you offer?**

CTA Click this link to join me in a 30-minute Masterclass where I show you exactly what to do and the questions to ask software customers

The Masterclass occurs live on Thursday July 15th at 10am Pacific time.

To your success,

YOURNAME

P.S. Here's the link again to join a 30-minute Masterclass on Thursday July 15th at 10am Pacific time.

I will show **you how you can make existing customers convince themselves to buy more of your products ...**

...without the need to sweat over preparing the perfect customer pitch.

3. Spotlight A New Feature Or Software Product Release

I used to be shocked at how few of our software features some of our customers adopted.

In fact, it somewhat scared me.

If they are not using our product to its full potential, could that mean we could lose them as customers?

But the bigger issue was "service".
If we had something that they could use but they just didn't know about it ....or never got around to using it because of its learning curve, that meant only one thing:

We were not helping our customers to the full.

Spotlighting a feature that customers care about is a great way to solve this problem... but what I love more about spotlighting is this:

Spotlighting a feature, that is focusing on that one feature in a communication, delivers a brilliant excuse to contact a customer and find out what they are doing.

In fact, there are so many great reasons to spotlight a feature.

WHEN can you spotlight a newish or key feature?

- Immediately after someone purchases your product...

  ... and for the first month, to increase their awareness of what your product can do for them

- At least every quarter to stay in touch and portray value
- When you need to revive a customer relationship
- Six months after you release a new feature.
- Reiterate and remind customers about its value and try to get them onboard.

- When the same question keeps cropping up during customer support's calls
- If a customer tells you how brilliant a feature is, then share the joy.
  Use their quote (without necessarily naming them) as the hook to your communication message to other customers in order to share the joy and usefulness of the feature

The best way to talk about a new or key product feature powerfully?

By discussing results that the feature creates, and by generating emotional desire for the feature.

Instead of describing FEATURE-BENEFIT information, use a more powerful approach. Describe this triplet.
A *feature*, the *results* that it gets and the professional and personal *desires* that the result meets.

FEATURE – RESULT – DESIRES

In the example that follows I will spotlight a feature of my product.

HOOK **What we learned from two customers who are using QuikSketch**

"Will it work?"

Was the question on my mind.

I was sweating with trepidation as we rolled out the beta version of our QuikSketch feature;

the culmination of 18 months of development.

The monetary cost of a mistake to our business was immense.... not to mention the horror of letting customers down if a feature didn't get the job done.

STORY You see, we are passionate about helping you get manufacturing production and shipments accomplished correctly and we know that you need to **model your own internal workflow and update it within the software.**

If you are a *QuikFlow* customer who asked for this feature because you wished to make adding to your workflow as simple as drawing on a piece of paper, then we wanted to **share what two of our 30 beta customers discovered when they tried QuikSketch for the first time.**

Customer "A" used QuikSketch to create new report automations:

CUSTOMER "A" had been accustomed to running production and shipping status reports every morning by hand, a tedious task.

They put QuikSketch to work to create automated manufacturing status and shipment reports.
They were able to set this up in less than 10 minutes.

They can now mail daily reports automatically to a company list.
A tireless worker whose job it had been to extract this data by hand and send these reports out at 6am every morning could, at last, get the sleep she deserved ... and **report recipients could count on those reports appearing like clockwork daily** at 6am !

STORY **Customer "B" used Quiksketch to add new product flow variants to their assembly process, each time they added a new product to their manufacturing production line:**

CUSTOMER "B" had a manufacturing workflow where status updates were entered daily by over 450 electronic scanners. **They use QuikSketch to manage order assembly, and shipment tracking.**

They were rolling out a new product in need of a different assembly process and they needed to track. They copied an existing assembly process tracker using the drag and drop feature in QuikSketch and then modified it to create a tracker for the new product..... all in less than 30 minutes.
In the past, they worried whether they had captured new manufacturing processes correctly. They were accustomed to a lot of testing and verification to ensure that all the tracking had been properly set up.

With QuikSketch, **they felt safe in the knowledge that their manufacturing process had been correctly modeled, ready to be put into use to track a new product down the assembly line.**

Testing showed this to be the case.

One Key Takeaway

Why exactly am I sending you this email?

Well, let me ask you …

Do you ever add new products to your workflow?

Do you worry every time you need to modify your workflow to meet a new need?

Are there tasks that you find tedious that you currently perform manually?

If yes, tune in to a 30-minute webinar where I'll show you how to get started on your path to automating this so you no longer have to worry about doing the task manually.

CTA

Please **click here to join me for this complementary 30-minute webinar.**
I will run it live on Wednesday, May 22 at 1pm Pacific time.

I will show you how to automate new report generation and save time when you add new manufacturing process trackers…
This will let you remove from your day tedious, boring tasks that are below your pay grade … by automating them.

To your success,

YOURNAME

P.S. Find out what 30 customers already know.
Sign up here for the complementary 30-minute QuikSketch webinar on how to automate report generation and save time adding manufacturing process trackers.

4. "Big Idea" Email To Change A Way Of Thinking.

(Remove An Objection, Create A New Belief)

This email replaces a customer's old and limiting belief, something that is causing them to resist buying, with a *new* belief.

In this email's story, the reader realizes that their *limiting belief is actually the cause of their pain.* When they remove that limiting belief, they can now find a solution.

Use this type of email to remove objections when you are *priming a sale.* Refer to Chapter 2 for more information on priming the sale

HOOK **Thinking you can't afford to automate your logistics is actually costing you money**

Most people think that automating their logistics is an expensive and time-consuming task .... but that *couldn't be further from the truth*.

Perhaps you tried before to automate, found that the software learning curve was huge, and, at the end of it all, the solution felt clunky. Your staff hated to use it.

I get it ... You can pay a college kid a low wage to have them take care of logistics manually and it works OK. But you are still a bit concerned about what will happen when your company grows. You worry that you are sitting on a ticking time bomb.

You have the occasional embarrassing human error that disgruntled a customer.

STORY And, truth be told, you really would love to have an automated system. I've been there, too.
My company grew profits by over 25% in one year and I literally could not keep up. I was left managing a team of college kids rather than working on the long-term improvements and hiring that my business desperately needed.

I tried a few software solutions, but the learning curve was so ridiculous that I ended up having to pay a consultant to create a customized solution that met our specific needs.
It took months and then the system would crash, such that I couldn't get the status of a customer's shipment.
It was not easy for my operators to use the system.

So I gave up

And then I discovered the *JIST product*. It took less than a day to install and learn.
Customer support walked me through basic training and helped me to set up the product in our factory in less than a day.

At last, **I could quit manually handling product shipments.**
I had shipment status at my fingertips.

One Key Takeaway

So let me ask you this.
Would you rather keep dealing with college kids and doing manual logistics or … use JIST and take care of logistics automation once and for all, with a simple, easy to use, quick to install system, all fully supported and backed 24/7 ?

CTA

If you would like to automate your logistics so that you actually can *grow* your business to the next level, without massive learning curves or complicated software, feel free to register here for our 45 minute webinar on August 23, at 10am Pacific Time

Sincerely,

YOUR NAME

P.S. **Register here for the webinar with live Q&A – In it we will show you how you can automate your logistics with JIST software.**

We will include five case studies that show you how easy it is to set up automated logistics and the results that our customers saw.

“BIG IDEA” Email Template

Use this template to create your “new-belief”-forming, objection removing email. You can use it to portray a “big idea” that you have

HOOK **Thinking you have no time to solve (PROBLEM) is (costing /| risking) (you/your) (money/ time / business)**

Most people think (ROADBLOCK / Belief that they don’t have enough time) … but that couldn’t be further from the truth.

Maybe you tried to fix this before and (this happened).

I get it… You do (painful thing) and it works OK, but you still worry about (PAIN).

It costs you (time, money, risk - Be specific, with numbers)…

…and you really would love to have (RESULT).

STORY Let me tell you the story about when I (hit the same PAIN/low point) and how that led to (RESULT that they want) and how much time was saved.

(At this point, follow the framework for creating a basic story in Chapter 6 where the main character overcame the same roadblock as your customer has. This is a counterexample to the person’s current belief and an illustration of why their old belief is false and limiting.
The story includes how people felt and conversation sound bites.

Story structure: CHARACTER-MISSION-STAKES-ROADBLOCK-RESULT)

One Key Takeaway	So let me ask you this. Would you rather keep having (PAIN) or purchase (MY PRODUCT) and get (RESULT)?
CTA	If you would like to fix (PAIN) , do this ____
	Sincerely
	(YOURNAME)
	P.S. Do this __ if you want to get rid of (PAIN) once and for all.

5. Email That Creates Connection, Revives An Old Customer Relationship, And Shows How Much You Care

In this type of email, we focus primarily on shared emotions, since this will result in our customer feeling similar to and connected to us.

The audience for this particular email example is a person who performs customer support.

HOOK **You became a customer support professional because you love to make a difference.**

STORY It was not that long ago that I had an epiphany. I was like you, faced with helping a customer to debug a difficult problem.

Then this happened**: For 5 long days, I couldn't reproduce the problem.** Back and forth with the customer trying different things .... I felt terrible for my customer since the bug had driven their project to a complete stand-still.

Then it dawned on me; A way that I could make things better.

What if I could achieve the equivalent of sitting and watching over their shoulder to see what they were doing when the bug occurred?
I contacted one of our development engineers and asked her to implement a debug mode that worked with remote desktops.

At first, it didn't give us the info we needed to reproduce hard bugs, but we kept trying new things to improve visibility into what was going on under the hood in our software when the bug arose.

We were finally able to get the very data we needed to see what our software error was and, at last, to reproduce the problem.

One Key Takeaway **You can do this too.**

What would it mean to you? How would you feel if you could get a faster turnaround on bug fixes or workarounds for your customer by being able to actively debug a problem as if you were at the customer's location, securely, yet from the comfort of your own desk?

CTA Click here if you would like to know how you, too, can do this.

To your success,

YOURNAME

P.S. If you would like to find out how to get fast turnarounds, fixing seemingly impossible to reproduce software bugs, click here.

CONNECTION Email Template

Here is the format that was used in the previous email example, and that you can adapt for your own emails to create a connection

HOOK **You became a (JOB TITLE) professional because you had (MISSION)**

It was not long ago that I had *another* epiphany.

STORY I was like you – I saw people in (PAIN).

Then this happened ___

(describe how you hit rock bottom, and elaborate on the ROADBLOCKS and how you felt. Be specific. Quote numbers)

And then it dawned on me that I could make things better.

So, I took (RESOURCES) and figured out how to get (RESULT)

At first, It didn't work ... but I kept working at it. And finally got (RESULT).

One Key Takeaway **You can get (RESULT), too.**
What would it mean to you... How would you feel if you could get (RESULT) for your customers, too?

CTA **Click here to get (RESULT).**

Sincerely,

YOURNAME

P.S. Want to fulfill your (MISSION) and get (RESULT). Click here to find out how.

6. Email To Demonstrate "How To" (Help Existing Customers. Show How You Solve A Customer's Problem)

This email example will show you how to offer a demo (demonstration) of a feature or workflow while motivating your audience to take you up on the offer!

It offers detail on how to solve a specific problem (in this example, the problem is how to make videos without spending hours doing it or encountering stage-fright)

The email's one key takeaway leaves the customer wanting more.

The result?

The customer will feel compelled to click on the link in the email to take you up on the offer of a demo.

HOOK **How any sales professional can get a video created in less than *one hour*, even if they can't write a script and flunked English at school.**

STORY Though most of us hate to admit it, we know that if we're teaching someone about a product, **a video will get a more enthusiastic response than any amount of text written about the very same topic.**

Yet we don't create videos because, if the topic takes more than a minute or so to discuss, we are a little bit scared that things might go wrong on camera.

You fire up the cellphone camera, run 5 takes, don't like what you see, and decide to give up and type an email instead.

Some of us even feel a bit embarrassed in front of a camera.

We reason that, even if we could solve this fear, we'd end up being long winded, sounding defocused, unless we write a script and just read it when we record our video.

But when we read from a teleprompter, we sound unnatural.

And then there is another problem.

Once the video is recorded, we fear that we are not technical enough to figure out how to edit it to make it really punchy ....

HINT: **You don't need to be able to edit videos at all**

I used to feel that way too, but one day I decided to take part in a video-making challenge.

Each day, for 30 days we would be given a title and assignment.

The daily assignment was to create a video that was less than five minutes in length.

On the first two days, it took me 20 or so recording attempts to get the video right. I kept reading from a teleprompter and the speed wasn't "right", or I would misread something, or even go "off script".

This was the wrong approach. For starters, it was fine to have a plan for what I was going to say but reading off a teleprompter was **just me trying to be perfect.**

I needed to create a mindset that would give me confidence to just speak naturally, without a script, to solve this problem once and for all.
I needed to sound more natural and authentic on camera.

One Key Takeaway

I discovered that I can look natural and unstressed on camera if you follow just three steps.

Step 1: Practice.
But how do you make sure that you get enough practice? Like me, you just have to make yourself create a video each day for 30 days.
Put it in your calendar and have an accountability buddy!
Practice will grow your confidence much sooner than you think.
For me, I saw a radical improvement by day five.
Practice for 30 consecutive days and, like me, at the end of the 30 days, and quite possibly sooner, you will get the video done in a single take.

Step 2: Create a list of topics ahead of time.
What myths do customers still believe that are, in fact, false?
What's changing in the industry?
Frequently asked questions?
Think of experiences that you have in common with customers, that will make you be seen as a human being, instead of a salesperson.
In other words, a topic that lets your customers know that you care.

Step 3: Use a "speaking to a friend" mindset to gain a confident and natural presentation style that people will love.
As you record, simply imagine that you are having a conversation in which you are *helping a friend.* Your conversational tone will sound natural and your demeanor authentic so that people immediately warm up to you.

CTA Need more help?

Click here to watch four short videos and download an action sheet that will walk you through the steps that you need to take to create your own videos, and eliminate your stage fright and painful video iterations.

Sincerely,
YOURNAME

P.S. Click here to watch four short videos that take you step-by-step through the simple process to overcome your stage fright and create "no-editing-required" videos for your customers in one take.

"HOW TO" Email Template

Here's the template that you can use to generate a similar "HOW TO" email

HOOK **How any (AUDIENCE) can get (RESULT) in (TIMEFRAME), even if (ROADBLOCK).**

STORY My customer / I was like you want to get (RESULT) but they ran into (ROADBLOCK). They thought that they would never solve it

And that, even if they could solve it, it would take too long, and besides... they were not technical enough to figure out with software that claimed to solve the (PROBLEM).

And, if you are like my customer, you haven't solved this (PROBLEM) either

So, I put this quick video/email together to help....
so that you can solve (PROBLEM) once and for all.

One Key Takeaway Here are the 3 steps that you need to take

Step 1: ____ Do ___ so that you can ____.

Step 2: ____ Do ___ so that you can ____.

Step 3: ____ Do ___ so that you can ____.

Need more help?

CTA *(Pick one of these or something similar)*

- Send me an email with your questions.
- Download the whitepaper / watch this video.
- Tell me what other topics you would like me to cover.

Sincerely,
YOURNAME

P.S. Take (NEXT STEP) to find out how to get (RESULT).

6. Show the Customer "How To" Do Something With A Quick Case Study Or Story

"HOW CAN I do ____ with your product?"

A frequent question that customers ask of you and your support team.

There are 2 ways to boost readership on a "How To" email.

Use a case study which frames the "how to" information with a story and thus makes it super interesting to follow.

Use a title ("hook") that builds curiosity and promises "What's In It For Me?" – What will your customer learn?

Instead of using a boring title such as "How To Solve (PROBLEM)"

You might, for example, use one of these

- o "What (CUSTOMER) taught me about solving (PAIN)."
- o "The real reason you have (PAIN) and how (CUSTOMER) FIXED IT."
- o "Understanding why (CUSTOMER) ditched (TRADITIONAL METHOD)
  will change how you think about (PROBLEM)"
- o "(CUSTOMER) thought they'd never get out of (PAIN) and then this happened."

Contrast these titles and the email template that I will show you next to a boring email that merely describes step-by-step
"How to solve (PROBLEM)" and risks boring folks to tears.

Example:

HOOK **Title: Understanding why (CUSTOMER-NAME) ditched TRADITIONAL one-to-one email marketing will change how you think about reaching out to customers.**

STORY What impression do you picture in your mind when you think about Apple or Microsoft?... Successful? Leading edge?

It wasn't always that way.

Take our customer (CUSTOMER-NAME).
When they started out, they had little revenue, no marketing budget and a lean sales team of just two people.
Their efforts were eclipsed by the development and marketing budgets of two large brand name competitors, Apple and Microsoft, who used their platform to squash smaller software competitors.

Luckily for (CUSTOMER-NAME), the world was shifting to online digital marketing instead of the traditional expensive TV, Radio and magazine ads.

They struggled to meet payroll, working remotely and out of the basement in the founder's parents' house.

This went on for over a year. They acquired two big customers.... and then lost them both.

Their expensive investment in acquiring and helping these customers; gone

But they knew that the software that they had was unique and believed in it.

And then this happened...

I happened to run into them at a networking event.

They told me how they had tried traditional marketing techniques and that they weren't working. The leads that they got were poor and their closing rate was only 10%.

They couldn't get venture funding because they couldn't demonstrate predictable revenue growth.

They showed me their software. They were right. I could see right away it was special; quicker, more scalable and intuitive than their competitors'.

So, I got to work to help them.

Using our software, we put together a digital marketing email sequence to nurture customers automatically.

We created an online sales funnel to educate and persuade customers, walking them closer and closer to a sale, whilst filtering out mismatches. This system captured leads and warmed up prospects *before* (CUSTOMER-NAME) called them so that the focus could be on closing them.

I know what you are thinking. You have the identical challenge, but it's too complicated to put together a digital marketing platform like this? And, even if you could, you don't know how to write emails that sell.

(CUSTOMER-NAME) believed the same thing.

The turning point was that traditional methods were failing... and they had to do something before they ran out of cash.

I helped them realize that **all they needed was a**

five-email sequence that you can customize from our swipe files and training: an online sales funnel, perfectly sequenced and written in the way that is perceived by customers as "teaching", not selling. Each email in the sequence warmed prospects up and drove them to the next sales step.

This warming up of customers gained them enthusiastic and qualified leads instead of cold ones that were going to be a long haul and often a waste of time to try and close.

In four short weeks, their close rate was up to 25% and it increased to 35% after they tuned their online funnel and emails.

They then put the system to work in a second way, to communicate with new customers and onboard them, so that they could avoid the second problem that they had had -- losing customers (a.k.a. "churn").
They saw churn drop by 50%, and stabilized at a 5% annual churn rate!

One Key Takeaway

If you want to get qualified customers on a very **low marketing budget** and think that there's a big learning curve, I understand.

(CUSTOMER-NAME) thought the same thing.

I want to share something with you. You can overcome your fears and **put a system in place using templates and swipe files that we provide.**

(CUSTOMER-NAME) realized they had a choice, keep grappling with low customer conversion rates and with losing customers... or solve it by investing in (MY PRODUCT/OFFER) to automate communication sequences – sequences that *trained* customers and prospects.

The results that (CUSTOMER-NAME) obtained were tremendous: 50% reduced churn rate and 25%+ increase in sales conversion rates.

CTA **If you are ready to fix high customer acquisition costs and churn problems with a systematic automated approach, click here to find out more.**

To your success,

YOURNAME

P.S. **If you sell software or services, find out how to automate getting qualified, warmed-up leads and end the tiresome process of wasted energy on tire kickers. Learn how you can use these same strategies to keep existing customers from jumping ship.**
Click here to find out more.

CASE STUDY TEMPLATE

Here's an email template to use. You have a choice of three case study hooks shown. Insert the problem or pain that your product solves for your customer where it says "PAIN":

HOOK

- **HOOK1: "(CUSTOMER) thought they'd never get out of pain and then this happened."**
- **HOOK2: "What (CUSTOMER) taught me about solving (PAIN)."**
- **HOOK3: "The real reason you have (PAIN) and how (CUSTOMER) fixed it."**

STORY Let me tell you a story about (CUSTOMER) who wanted (RESULT).

They had (PAIN). They wanted to get rid of it once and for all,

so they could achieve (RESULT/STAKES *e.g.: ROI, less stress, lower risk, identity).*

They tried (Path of failure that others also find make them fail),

but they were stuck for over a year because they believed (ROADBLOCK).

Many of you in (PAIN) can probably relate to this feeling.
You are probably thinking that you have that same problem.
My customer hit (LOW POINT) and they decided that something had to change, so they tried (SOLUTION).

I know what you're thinking. You have (ROADBLOCK). (CUSTOMER) believed the same thing. *(Tell the story of all the things the customer tried… the pain they felt… and then finally, the customer's turning point.)*

I helped them discover how to get (RESULT/ TRANSFORMATION)

and now they have (RESULT).

One Key Takeaway If you want (RESULT) and think that you can't overcome (ROADBLOCK), I understand.

(CUSTOMER) thought the same thing.

I want to share with you that you absolutely can overcome (ROADBLOCK).

(CUSTOMER) realized that they had a choice. Stay in (PAIN) or solve (PROBLEM) by investing in (MY PRODUCT/OFFER)

The results that they saw were ___ .

CTA If you are ready to solve (PROBLEM), (DO THIS)

(e.g., reply to this message, schedule a meeting in my calendar… etc.)

Sincerely,
YOURNAME

P.S… If you are a (TYPE OF CUSTOMER) that has (ROADBLOCK) and wants (RESULT), do this ___ to get (SOLUTION).

7. Offer A Freebie To Gauge Interest

Such As A Whitepaper, PDF Download, Webinar, Masterclass, Training

This email template can be used to sign up customers for a webinar, masterclass or training event, or to persuade them to download a white-paper or PDF file.

It is a **great way to generate an email list of people interested in a very targeted webinar or whitepaper topic** and thus sort out the wood from the chaff as far as who **is interested in something that is a particular strength of your product.**

The email urges people to "sign up" for the freebie by creating curiosity.
It then tells a compelling story that increases the chance that the customer will show up or download.

Contrast this fun email and its template to a boring email that simply says
"Sign up for our webinar. In it you will learn...."

How is our email different?

The email creates emotional desire and excitement about the webinar so that people are likely to read the email, sign up and show up. It uses a variant of a story that I used earlier in this book.

This time I use the story to preface an important point about how to get attention and keep it, something that I will teach about in the free giveaway that the email offers.

HOOK **Five ways to get an audience's attention: Sign up for a free Whitepaper/Free Training/ Masterclass before midnight Friday.**

STORY Back in high school, I admit that, toward the end of the day, I used to clock watch.

Anticipation that I could get home and play with my friends?
Well, yes…

But the main reason I found myself clock-watching was *fatigue*… after hours sitting in the classroom.

The later and longer that session progressed, the less I remembered.

But there was one subject, Physics, where I would listen intently and remember it vividly afterwards, even when the lesson occurred in the last hour of the school day.

The way that it was taught gave me so many big "a-ha" moments.

I could immediately relate and apply what I learned in that class to everyday life.

Talk about the concept of inertia and I could relate that to the difficulty getting going on my bike after I stopped at a traffic light.

Talk about gravity and I could relate that to dropping a ball
or to videos of how light astronauts walking on the moon for the very first time felt as they effortlessly bounced around in their heavy space suits, as if jumping around on an inflated bouncy castle.

One Key Takeaway My point?

If you want people to read your messages and remember what you said, even when they are tired and grumpy.
And even if you think your topic is the most complicated one they have heard today, then paint pictures and stories in their head of your customers.
Stories that relate directly to your topic;

There is a specific way to do this.

That special way and how you can replicate it in your emails is revealed in a *complementary* whitepaper / masterclass / onboarding / training.

CTA But you need to sign up here before midnight Friday.

To your success,

YOURNAME

P.S. **Here's the <u>FREE masterclass/whitepaper/training link</u>** for you to learn how to **keep a customer's attention so that you can sell them more.**

Be sure to **<u>sign up</u> before Friday at midnight**, whereupon the FREE masterclass/whitepaper/training will go "poof" and turn into a pumpkin.

8. Find Out What Your Customer Is Doing (so that you can offer very specific help and sell more)

"What are you working on?" and
"How are things going?"

Ask many a busy customer this via an email.... and there is a good chance that they will ignore you – Why would they take their precious time to respond unless they have a burning reason?

Yet here is an email example that asks a customer to respond to these questions
and that will get you a response.

Why? Because it shows the customer that empathy is the reason that you are asking. After all, they too have customers.

The visibility that you get when you send out such an email will both let you help your customer and find opportunities to make incremental sales

How do I get empathy and a response?

In the example, my email first engages the customer with a story, to articulate why customer feedback has always been helpful to me personally in the past. This lets the customer comprehend the depth to which I truly care. And makes them realize that the same is true of their relationship with their customers

That it is not me demanding their time but that I have their interests in mind.

The story makes me appear human, predisposing the customer to respond.

Contrast this example to a boring email that says "How are things going?"...

HOOK **TITLE: I asked this one question, and it saved my business.**

STORY In 1999, when I was the business development manager for set top box semiconductor chips that power your TV with satellite and cable livestreams, I would visit broadcasters to understand new needs that lay on their horizons.
Our turnaround time on implementing anything new in chip hardware was at least 18 months; including six months for delivering software that ran with the hardware.

The cost of rolling out a new version of the chipset (that is, the cost of a mistake if we got it wrong), was multi-millions of dollars in manufacturing costs alone.

Worse, being several months late to market because we had to correct a mistake, amounted to tens of millions of dollars in lost opportunity cost.

So, there I sat, in front of broadcast engineers, a sketch of a prototype for our next generation chipset on the screen and I asked them,

"Will this do what you need?" and,

"What else do you need?"

Whereupon they began suggesting performance enhancements and other functional features that they needed ....and .... they detailed why.
Putting a prototype "strawman design" in front of them always drove excellent feedback, because it is easier for someone to critique a proposal than to remember to describe the inner details of what they want in the first place.

But do you know what drove the very best feedback of all?

The best feedback occurred when I asked,

"Could you give me an example of how you would use that feature so that I can understand WHY you are asking for it"
I was asking for a "Use Model"

"Please give me an example!!"

This question alone saved my business time and time again. This was because I now **implemented** in my first new release of the chipset **exactly what the customer *meant* that they needed**, not my interpretation of what they were asking for.

Understand the "use model", and you will implement the true intent.

In a competitive chip business, getting it right the first time amounted to saving my business. It saved me from being beaten to market by a competitor.

One Key Takeaway

So, why is this point important to your business?

Because I know that you have the same problem – A need to know what your customers really think, what they need and why.

I am here to help you get done what you really need to get done; to understand exactly why you need new capabilities in our product and how you would use them to deliver benefits to your customers.
To find out about the little things in the product that cause you major amounts of annoyance.

CTA **So let me ask you this,**

"What irritates you about our software and why?"

"What stops you from getting the job done with our software, and why?"

"How do you use it? "

Reply to this email to let me know how I can help.

To your success,
YOURNAME

P.S. Let me know how things are going and what I can do to help.
Maybe we already have something that you need such as free training, but perhaps we did a bad job in not letting you know.

No feedback is too small !!

Or maybe I need to get our magical engineers to implement something in the software, so that you will sing when you don't have to contend with some irritating thing 20 times a day or pilot errors that occur because you are doing something manually.
Just let me know what you are trying to get done ... and why ...

Reply to this email, and I'll be happy to help.

A couple things to note about the previous example:

1. I use a story (what is called a "key point story"), to make the customer understand **why it matters to me personally that I help them; that I care** because, "I get how important" even one small improvement to our software can be to your business.
2. The main body of this email is, in fact, the CTA, the reason to respond.
   Open-ended questions that give them a reason to reply to you work great.
   I want them to reply because it will accomplish two things:

- Start a conversation
- When they reply, the fact that they respond will cause their mail system to keep me out of their SPAM Folder in future.
  I become a trusted person in *their* eyes, too.

3. I give them something.
   I teach them the importance of use models, something that they can use with *their* customers.
   I do this so that I create "reciprocity", a powerful persuasion technique that tends to make someone want to give you something in return.

   I teach them a useful life lesson to follow up with an answer from a customer with the question "Why?"

   My giving my customer something upfront then generates a willingness to give me something in return.

   If I had just asked something of them (their time) without offering anything in return, I would not have been successful.

4. I repeat the CTA in the P.S. in case they "skip read" the email.

Your Email Checklist

Now that you have seen some email examples, let's review exactly what I did.
What caused the reader to read the email and to take action?

I make my customer *feel* something.

"People don't remember what you say,
they remember how you make them feel" - I...:

- Used vivid and colorful words
- Talked about how I felt and what I was thinking (pain, drain, fear, joy, elation)
- Told stories so that the audience *"lived an experience"* with me.
    - My story made customer feel my pain and joy.
    - My story may include data in it (e.g., a case study) or it may purely be a tale that illustrates an important point

A Story will increase the message's impact by demonstrating:

- **Empathy** – How you have been there
- **Roadblocks/emotional fears** they need to overcome (amplify the pain) and how to solve them
- **A new way/insight** that solves a problem that matters and **the result**
- **What solving a problem will mean** to the customer emotionally
    - Why it matters
    - A vision
    - A transformation

- **What's at stake if they do or don't act** and thus they have a choice to make.

The email accommodates the "Two Reader Paths"

(The "skip" reader and "long-form" reader)

- Even the "skip" reader receives the key message and can tell what action to take.

Quick and easy reading

- Use **small words**, e.g. instead of "increase", use the words "rise", "gain", "jump", "soar".
- I **"let it breathe"**
  - o Short sentences
  - o One-sentence paragraphs
  - o Lots of white space on the page
- An "**easy-to-read" font**, such as Helvetica, Calibri, Arial

Reads the same way that I would speak

- May include dialog and characters for easier, more entertaining reading

Has a Thumb-stopping title

- Creates **Curiosity** and articulates "What's In It For Me" (**WIIFM**)
- Is either a question, or makes them want to know more, or creates a Cliffhanger

Has One Key Takeaway

- Takeaway **appears in Bold** text so that "skip" readers will not miss it.
  To check that you did this, ask yourself "If the bold-faced text is all that the customer reads, would they get the gist of the message?"

- **Is about the customer, not me.** Its whole point is to describe their *pain*, and what is at stake and make them think "Yes, that's me!"
- It makes it clear what **buying vs. missing out means** to them personally and professionally.

Has a SINGLE Call To Action (CTA)

- Includes, **in bold,** the single thing that you want the customer to do next
- **Repeats the CTA in a P.S.**
- **Makes the CTA easy to take**
(e.g., includes an enticing button or link)

Summary

Perhaps it takes you over 10 minutes to compose a complex email to a customer, yet how can you make sure that it will be read?

Today, you are fortunate if 15-20% of your emails are consumed if the recipients don't know you well.

If you can't get customers to open your email then they will not take action on it for sure.

How can you get customers to consume your emails AND TAKE ACTION.

Or put quite simply, how are you going to fill webinars, get people to show up for presentations, move forward with an evaluation, or have a customer respond to your offer?

Sure, you can try using the phone but it really comes down to this: you need to get the customer's attention and then know how to *keep* it.
You then need to drive them to a specific action.

It starts with getting a customer to click on the email to open it. Then make the content interesting and easy for customers to both consume and take action on.

A well-constructed email such as those in this chapter will keep the customer relationship alive, even if your customer isn't immediately ready to buy more from you.

Follow the abbreviated email checklist on the next page to achieve connection with your customers.

Abbreviated Email Checklist

- Email Includes:
    - o **Thumb-Stopping Hook** (HEADLINE) – So that customer opens the email.
        - ■ Delivers curiosity & promises WIIFM (What's In It For Me)
    - o A **Story** with character, stakes, big roadblock and results
        - ■ … that makes customers feel something
    - o **One key takeaway**, the one thing I want customers to remember
    - o One Strong **CTA** (Call To Action) or Offer – The one thing you want customers to do next.
        - ■ A **CTA that is easy to take** - **A button, or link** and
        - ■ A **P.S. that repeats the CTA**
- Is **About My Customer And What They Need**
    - ■ **Connects** with the customer as a person
    - ■ **Changes a belief** to remove a common objection or roadblock or inspires them with a "big idea"
    - ■ How another customer **solved a problem and got a specific result**
- Two reader paths: **long-form, and for the "skip reader"** (Refer to Chapter 12)**.**
- **Quick and Easy Reading**
    - o Short words
    - o One sentence per paragraph
    - o White space
- **Write like you speak**

Chapter 11

Fix Your Boring Presentations

Create High Impact Presentations, Masterclasses and Webinars

"The best and most beautiful things in the world cannot be seen or even touched—they must be felt with the heart."

—Helen Keller

It was 3pm on a Thursday and, with pleasantries completed, a meeting with a company whose products complemented ours had just started.

This company's goal was to persuade mine to integrate our software with theirs. In concept, I had warmed to the idea over the phone since there was mutual customer demand.

But there was a problem.

I had some business-related questions that I asked to be addressed at the meeting. I also wished to understand this company's financial viability, mission and commitment to the cause.

Instead, in the meeting, I found myself bombarded with what looked like a customer presentation about the features of their product and how great it was.

After repeatedly trying to course-correct the meeting, to little avail, I began sliding glances towards my phone screen, checking email.
My mind wandered to a project that I had to complete by tomorrow.

I caught myself looking at the clock. The meeting ended after an hour without a clear follow up next step planned, since I had not received what I needed from the presentation.

This company had lost my attention within the space of the first 10 minutes.

With the workday over, at 7pm that night I headed to the movies with a friend.

75 minutes into the movie plot, we were both hanging off the edge of our seats as the tale crescendo'ed to its conclusion.

And then I got thinking.

How come the movie had kept me glued to the screen for 75 minutes, cellphone firmly planted in pocket, while the earlier meeting presentation had barely held my attention for 10 minutes?

What was the critical difference?

It was in how the information had been structured.
The movie had made use of a story structure. Its story line was easy, not difficult, to follow. It has tons of conflict to keep me in a state of anticipation. At the conclusion it resolved, the ending giving me closure.

If the partner presentation had used stories about customers needing the integration that the company sought.
If it had included an origin story about the partner company and why their mission mattered to them and was meaningful for their customers, I, for one, would have been hanging off my seat (I geek out on helping customers).

If they had messaged to me one reason why I personally should care and then wrapped it up with a suggestion of how we might move forward, the meeting would have been successful for us both.

We would have connected.

In this chapter, I will show you how to integrate your inner movie into your presentation, using a story.

Do this and you will keep the attention of those watching so that they receive and remember your message.

We will use the entire Sell Bigger Framework:

Pattern Interrupt – Hook – Story – One Key Takeaway – Offer/CTA

That is, your HIGH IMPACT PRESENTATION, MASTERCLASS, WEBINAR will be structured like this:

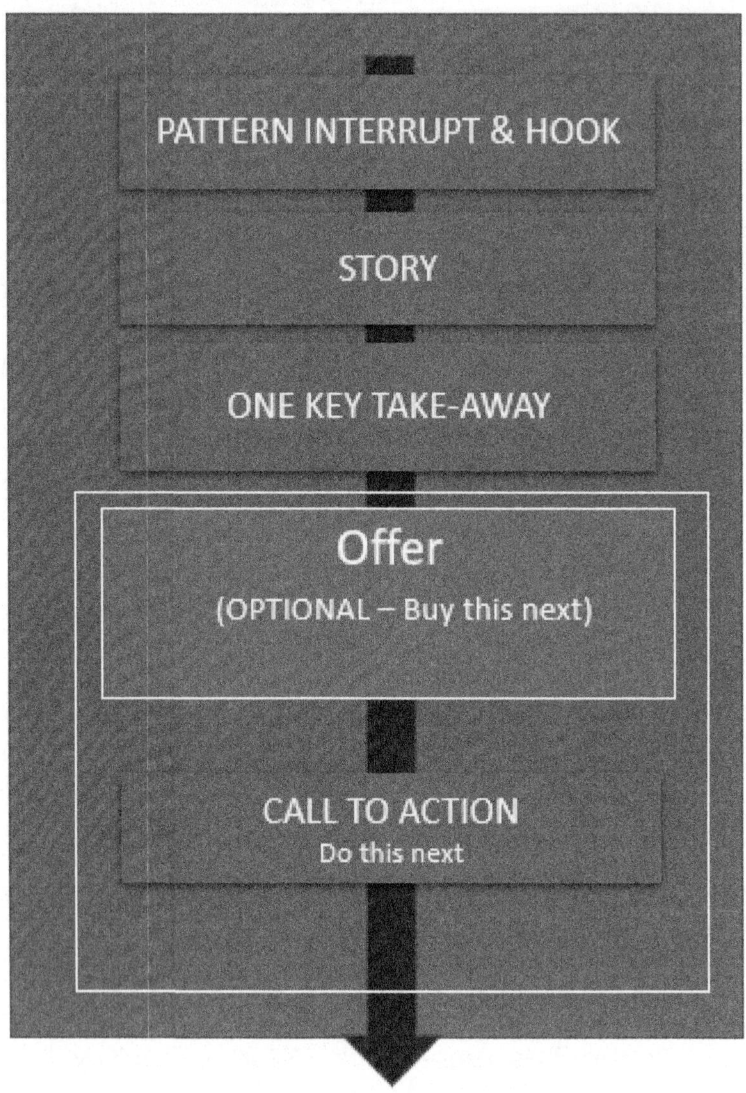

The Pattern Interrupt And Hook

Even though you already have the attention of people who have shown up to your presentation, that attention can rapidly wane.

For this reason, you need something in your presentation that stands out as a reason to pay attention – Something that creates curiosity and explains WIIFM

- a **hook and a pattern interrupt**

In a presentation, a pattern interrupt might be:

- A funny quote or cartoon to make your audience laugh
- A video clip

In a presentation, the hook could be:

- A picture that grabs attention
- A question to which the customer wants an answer
- A cliffhanger statement that makes the customer want to know more

To find your presentation's hook, consider the following:

- A key question or problem that customers have
- What is one difficult problem that your product solves?
- What's unique about your presentation?
- Why your presentation matters and is relevant to your customer
- What does it means to the audience personally and professionally to be more competitive, feel less risk, save time, get greater performance with your product; how will it make them feel?

TIP: Save ideas for future headline and hooks instantly in Trello (or other mobile note-making software)... Do this when:

- A customer asks a question
- You hear a quote that is meaningful to your customers
- You find a selling point that resonates with a group of customers

The Story

Who doesn't love a story?
The very most memorable presentations will have stories dotted along the way that make the customer smile about something or identify with the experience of the person in the story .... The story will cleverly create an emotional picture in the mind of the audience.

There are 6 types of story that you might consider for your presentation. I delve into these in greater detail in my training courses, yet they all share a format described in Chapter 3. The 6 types of story are:

1. **Origin Story**
    a. Your Company's beginnings
    b. Your "why?", MISSION & VISION driving your passion to serve customers
2. **Case Study**
    a. "A customer like you" story and result
3. **Overcoming Objection Story**
    a. Counter-example story
    b. A story about a "big idea"
    c. A new belief-forming story (that subtly gets rid of old misconceptions and objections)
4. **Product Story**
    a. "Behind the scenes" story that reveals what inspired a new product or feature
    b. Workshop creation story
    c. Feature creation story. The ups and downs of doing it right. A new product "reveal" story

5. **"Free PR" Stories that create Connection**

   This story could be any one of these things:

   a. Product release story – The genesis or inspiration behind a new feature and why it is important to you to help customers
   b. Why helping customers matters to individuals in your company.
   c. Mistakes I made and what I learnt.
   d. "Point of View" or Vision story

6. **"Key Point" Story**

   a. This is a paragraph that leads into and illustrates the main point of your presentation via an analogy or closely related topic.
      For example, this can be a tale from a movie, a daring act, or a quote from someone famous.
   b. Or it can be an unexpected occurrence that poses a similar question to the main topic of your communication
      I absolutely love to use this kind of thing as the opening of an email because it is short and memorable

TIP: If you think it will be tough to find stories, worry not! Create an online **"story vault"** in an application such as *Trello*. Place stories there as they come to mind and at the end of every day.
Refer to Chapter 6 to create your story ideas.

Note down a story in your online Story Vault when:

- Something pivotal happens to you
- A "teaching moment" with family and friends occurs in which you learn something new

- When you dared to do something that you were afraid to do
- You procrastinated about something and got around to doing it
- You see a movie or read a book where someone overcomes a roadblock that has a parallel to what your customer is trying to do, or to their fears
- Cases where a customer struggled or disbelieved that a solution existed to their problem, and then saw success with your solution, even if there were bumps in the road.

One Key Takeaway

Let me ask you this.

If there was one message that you wanted your customer to remember after the presentation, what would that be?
This one thing is your One Key Takeaway (yes, just one) that your presentation should include.

As mentioned in Chapter 7, this will be one of 3 things

1. A Big Idea / "A-ha" moment
2. A learning moment (Key Feature, Its Results and the Desires that it meets)
3. A case study that messages "it works"

Let's assume that the one key takeaway is a learning moment.

To construct your one key takeaway in a way that is compelling follow two steps:

<u>STEP 1</u>: Decide upon a top level feature or group of features that deliver one result when a customer uses your product

For that FEATURE write down:

- The RESULT that customers want when they use it Specifically, what does the feature help customers to avoid or gain?
- The DESIRES – that the result satisfies?

What do I mean by "Desires"?
I mean that you should ask yourself how your customer will *feel* when their problem is fixed? The desire is generally one of these 6 things

1. **Pain Relief.** How it will *feel* to get out of pain
2. **Status/Identity Increase**: How RESULT *reinforces your customer's values or who they strive to be*. How RESULT enables them to be part of a group

3. **Specialized/Specific Solution**: The *security* of knowing that your offering caters to their specific problem in their specific market
4. **Great Experience** with your product**:** How *pleasant* the journey of using your product will feel. The pleasure of great customer support, for example.
5. **New Opportunity:** The *confidence* of being able to solve their problem in a way makes them more competitive, more efficient etc.
6. **Bigger Reason**: How your solution will *service the customer's greater mission, personally and spiritually* (for example, a community benefit, more family time)

STEP 2:

Create Your One Key Takeaway.

Your One Key Takeaway is the **"Feature – Result – Desires**" combination that you created in Step 1.

Use the Action Sheet on the next page to note this down

Your Presentation/Webinar/Masterclass's One Key Takeaway (ACTION SHEET)

Fill in the form to create your one key takeaway

FEATURE NAME:

RESULT:

So you can ___
Or ...So you can avoid ___
Or ... Which helps you to ___

DESIRES:

Which means that ...

1. **PAIN RELIEF**
2. **STATUS / IDENTITY**
3. **SPECIALIZED / SPECIFIC**
4. **GREAT EXPERIENCE**
5. **NEW OPPORTUNITY**
6. **A BIGGER REASON**

Reinforce Your One Key Takeaway

In Chapter 9, we discussed three ways to talk about a topic. They are:

- **How To** - Solve a problem with a feature (Feature – Result – Desires triplet)
- **Big Idea** (Replace a customer's old belief with a new belief. This lets the customer visualize a new opportunity , and it is often used to remove an objection, founded in a misconception or old way of thinking)
- **Connection** (Illustrate that you care about your customer's problem and why. Prove that you care and your solution works using customer quotes, stories, and testimonials)

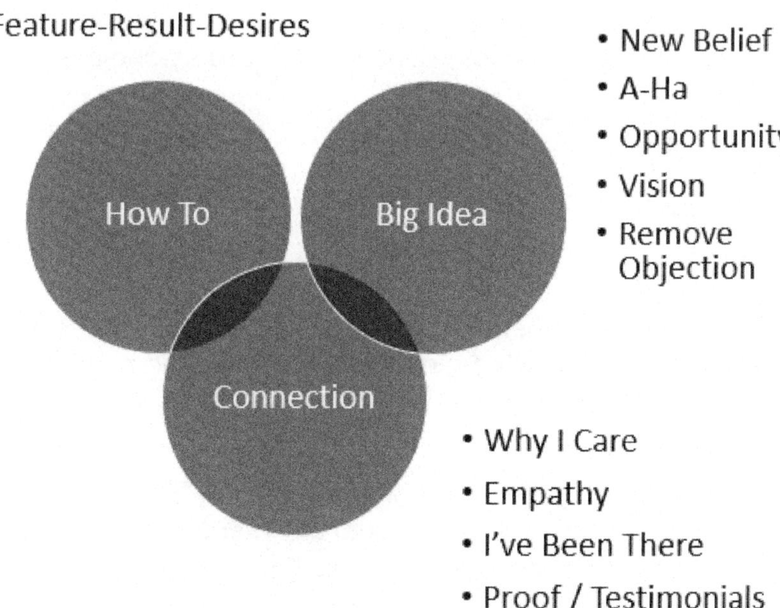

Include the three ways of communicating to reenforce the one key takeaway of your presentation, for example:

- **How To:** Show the approach used to solve a customer problem (and how it feels to solve it)
- **Big Idea:** Paint a vision of what is possible in order to overcome an objection
- **Connection:** Show how much you care using a case study as proof.

The Call To Action (CTA)

As you approach the end of your presentation, is it clear what the customer's "next step" should be?

Always make your presentation "actionable" by including a call to action and an optional offer.

Some best practices.

- Make that next step a **SINGLE next step** so that the customer does not become paralyzed by choices
- Make it **easy to do**
- Make it **as urgent as you can** (a deadline or genuine reason to act now)

Examples of a presentation CTA are:

- **Get started here with ___** ....
  e.g. To get started, enroll in this complementary on-boarding training/an evaluation/ a five-day challenge
- **Sign up.**
  e.g., sign up here for a workshop.
  Sign up with your email address in order to receive a freebie PDF document or training.

- **Do this right away**
  e.g., "Write down a situation where you can use this to solve (PROBLEM)"

  "Put this FREE action sheet to work"

- **A link or button with an Action in it.**
  Use this when you are distributing a copy of your slides

  e.g., → Yes – I want BENEFIT

- **A reason to act now**
  What the customer stands to lose if they don't act.
  How they will be out of pain right away if they do act.
  e.g., A deadline. How much they are losing each week by not acting

Examples of CTA text to use in your presentation

- *Take (this step) right now to get started*
- *Go here to register for a complementary whitepaper (This tactic allows you to collect email addresses of those seriously interested).*
- *Go here to add the next meeting to your calendar*
- *Let's meet with main contacts for proceeding forward with an evaluation or the trial*
- *Buy now.*
  20% Discount if you register within the next 24 hours
- *Be sure to register for this (EVENT) before (DEADLINE)*
- *Join our FREE User Group Community.*
- *We'd love you to register for this event.*
  Complementary tickets are available only to those who register today.

Your CTA may also include a sales offer.

The Offer

Here is how to present your offer within your presentation.

Refer to the Offers section of Chapter 8 for more details.

STEP 1: Prime the offer

- Subtly raise the most common objections and then alleviate each.
  "You are probably thinking (OBJECTION). Let me show you .... (SOLUTION or TOOLS) that take care of that"
- Empathize, "I've been there" and then...
- Show examples of customers who had doubts about their own personal ability to get results and succeeded in spite of this.
- Amplify the pain and thus the urgency of fixing their problem
- Make them laugh with a personal story about how you yourself didn't take action and how that worked out (not!) – Some self-deprecation goes a long way.

STEP 2: Make Your Offer

An important point – Sell the *offer*, not just your *product*.

For example:

Your OFFER =

Your Software

+

Results creators

24/7 customer support

Swipe files

Free Training

+

Urgency creators

Free ticket to our user conference next month

Concierge service to get your first design finished

+

Objection removers

Translator to import your design from Competitor software and verify it. (Objection: High Switching cost)

3-pay payment plan (Objection: too expensive)

Working case studies that you can use to improve and model your own (Objection: Too complicated to set up)

If you would like help in creating an offer around your product, so that your product appears larger than life and differentiated, please refer to my online training modules.

A presentation that primes and presents an offer will look like this

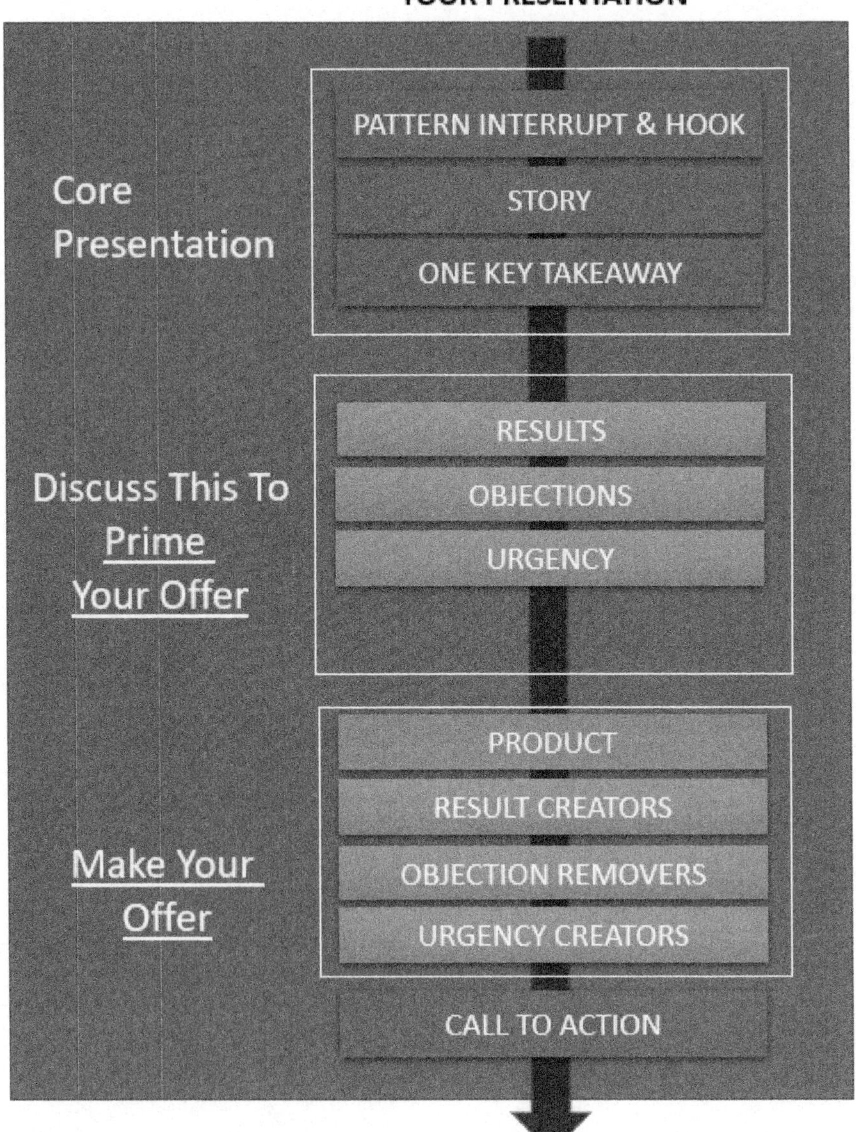

YOUR PRESENTATION/WEBINAR/ MASTERCLASS BLUEPRINT

PATTERN INTERRUPT (OPTIONAL)

Unusual Thing That Captures The Eye

(e.g., Picture or video snip that customer can self-identify with)

HOOK

Presentation Title And Intro

What's In It For Me? What Makes Them Curious?

(e.g. A cliffhanger question, a question customers always have, something that makes them want to know more and pay attention)

STORY

Origin Story, Key Point Story, Case Study, Product Story, Connection Story, Overcoming Objection Story, Point Of view/Vision/Behind the scenes/My big mistake)

ONE KEY TAKEAWAY

Feature – Result – Desires, Big Idea, I Care

CALL TO ACTION

SINGLE thing that you want them to do next

(e.g., Register for an evaluation here. Watch video. Join User Group Community)

OFFER (OPTIONAL)

PRODUCT + URGENCY + OBJECTION REMOVERS + RESULTS CREATORS

Here is an example:

PATTERN INTERRUPT (OPTIONAL)	**Unusual Thing That Captures The Eye**	Salesperson throwing their computer in a trash can in frustration
HOOK	**Presentation Title And Intro** **What's In It For Me? What Makes Them Curious?**	Why people ignore your emails and what to do about it
STORY	**Origin Story, Key Point Story, Case Study, Product Story, Connection Story, Overcoming Objection Story, Point Of View/Vision/Behind the scenes/my big mistake)**	Customer quit using my software when a competitor had a feature that we also had but customer didn't know we had... I had told them about the feature at least 10 times via email .. But they didn't even open my emails because they thought I was trying to pitch them rather than help them. My email headlines sucked ...
ONE KEY TAKEAWAY	**Feature – Result – Desires, Big Idea, I Care**	Feature: Email Writing Framework People look forward to my communications (RESULT)– Makes me feel like I can serve my customers better (DESIRE). Can now be with my family (DESIRE) and not sweat over last-minute deals late into the night at quarter end (RESULT)
CALL TO ACTION	**SINGLE thing that you want them to do next**	Register for my 30- minute Live Masterclass on May 21, 2021
OFFER (OPTIONAL)	**PRODUCT + URGENCY + OBJECTION REMOVERS + RESULTS CREATORS**	Start a FREE two-week trial and get these bonuses that you can keep no matter whether you continue or not

What if my customer doesn't stay until the end of my presentation?

Since the CTA traditionally appears near the end of the presentation, webinar or masterclass, how will the early departers know what to do next?

There are two additional things that will get those who leave early to none-the-less take the next step:

1. **Communicate a reason to stay:**

- **An extra reward for staying**
  Promise an extra bonus that will be announced at the end that will not be included in the webinar replay.
- **Prizes to those that ask questions at the end**
  "Must be present to win"
- **Pose a cliffhanger question at the beginning**
  Promise to answer that question near the end of the presentation
- **Promise that there will be a live Q&A or mystery speaker at the end.**

2. **Launch a follow-up email sequence to all attendees:**

Take the list of all attendees and send them all an email follow-up to drive people to your call to action and offer.

Your five-message follow up email sequence might look something like this:

1. Here's the replay link + one key takeaway + story that introduces one of the main webinar concepts
2. Story + summary of a piece of the presentation.
3. A "connection" story relevant to your presentation's one key takeaway … I was just like you encountering (PROBLEM) with (DOUBTS) and this is what I did
4. A "case study" story
5. Your offer

Summary

I found the inspiration for how to deliver a presentation from all that is good about the movies.

Just as in the movies, it was about keeping people glued to the screen for well over an hour, all whilst making a lasting impression.

We know for a fact that attention can be kept for over an hour because it's done in the movies every day.

How do we do this in a presentation?
By using these five elements:

1. A **Pattern Interrupt** such as a quote, fast action embedded video or cartoon to catch the eye
2. A **Hook** – A title that grabs attention by creating curiosity and talking about what is in it for your customer to listen.
3. A **Story** to keep the customer hanging on the edge of their seat. Use the story to overcome common objections, often without the customer even realizing that this is what you are doing.
4. There's really only one top level message: **One Key Takeaway**. If you keep it simple, your presentation will be remembered and listened to.
5. Always end the presentation with a next step: A **Call To Action and an optional Offer**.
   The offer, if presented, specifically drives customers to buy within a set timeframe. It removes objections by including line items that allay the customer's fears and accelerate early results.

In a webinar or masterclass, you want to give the listener a reason to stay to the end and have an email follow-up sequence.

Use webinars and masterclasses frequently to give your existing customers more input and seed interest in additional purchases.

Chapter 12

Fix Your Yawner of An Article, Journal or Whitepaper

Create High Impact Articles, Journals And Whitepapers

"In a noisy and disruptive era, no one owes you their attention."

—Bernard Kelvin Clive

Hands down, whitepapers and webinars have been my two best sources of high quality leads for semiconductor design software sales.

This was true whether I was looking for new customers that fit .... or for existing customers that I wished to keep happy and upsell.

It made sense that I would get great leads from articles and whitepapers

After all, the article and whitepaper "niched down", that is, it laser focused on a specific topic, It discussed a *very specific problem* that my software solved or a shift in the industry that was leading to a change that my software conveniently addressed.

By doing this, it *attracted the very customer that I wanted* – one who had a problem that my software solved.

But there was a problem.

When I talked to customers that had downloaded a whitepaper from my website, they would frequently ask me a question that was directly answered in the whitepaper.

It turned out that they hadn't read much more than a few early paragraphs plus the tables and figures.

I did my very best to be patient, and re-answer the question. Frankly, I was grateful that the whitepaper had been a conversation starter.

But I really wasn't satisfied with the situation.

My goal was to get the whitepaper to do a brilliant pre-qualification of these customers so as to not waste my sales team's time on sales calls that were destined to go nowhere.

In my ideal world, the whitepaper should build desire for my software, before the customer and I even talked on the phone.

It could only do that if the customer read the important bits that contained my message.

Yet few customers were doing this. Why was this?

Published articles or journal papers?

The problem was even bigger.

I could not tell who had read them and was not guaranteed a sales lead at all.

How was I going to get readers to consume the article or journal and then feel compelled to contact me?

The truth?

The only control I had upon whether an article or journal led to a sales engagement was in the way that I wrote the journal paper or article.

I needed to write in a way that got my message across even if the viewer only glanced at it for 10 seconds.

And, more importantly, I needed to incentivize readers **to take a very clear action** after they read it.

What Most Authors Do That Guarantees People <u>Won't</u> Read Their Article, Journal or Whitepaper ...

Think for a minute about your own experience as a consumer of articles and whitepapers.

Have you ever downloaded a whitepaper, or clicked to view an article and then, sigh, you discover that it is <u>*three screens long*</u>... and, gasp, most of it is textual ...

Is it going to be a good or a boring read?

Do you *scan* it first to assess whether it's worth your time?

Yet, at some time in your past, there was a 200-page long book that you simply couldn't put down because it enthralled you.

What's the difference between boring and enthralling?

As in presentations and emails ... it is the *story* that the article contains.

But even if you have a story, there is another challenge.

People think they don't have much time to read, especially when the content (an article, journal or whitepaper) is self-serving, and involves no interaction with a human.

I'll just "skip read" it for now

Is a common reaction from customers.

There are in fact two "reader paths" that you need to consider when you write. These are:

- Reader path for the rare person that reads it all - the *"long-form reader"*, and
- Reader path for the person who scans - the *"skip reader".*

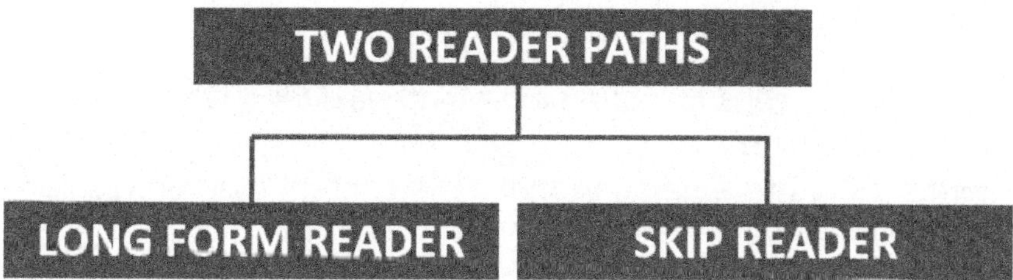
TWO READER PATHS
LONG FORM READER
SKIP READER

The Two Reader Paths

You spend weeks sweating over materials for a whitepaper, journal or article,
Iterate 10 or more times to make the content look professional and bullet-proof.
It's jam-packed with help and value.
It looks aesthetically fantastic.

The somber truth?
Most customers that download a whitepaper won't read much of it

What have most authors failed to do?

Most authors have failed to write for their biggest audience - the "skip reader".

Here's what your skip reading customer will do.

They will first scan the content to decide whether your prose is worth a closer look.

Which leads to my question.

What can you do to pique the interest of the customer's scanning eyes so that they decide to read on?

Let's think for a moment:
When you skip read, where do your eyes gaze first?

Your eyes tend to first drift to these places:

- Headline and subheadings
- The first sentence of the paper/article/journal
- The last paragraph
- Figures and figure titles
- "Callouts" such as quotations, bullets, or bold face text

Bingo....

Writing For The Skip Reader

To cater to the skip-reader, therefore, the entire message, that is the

PATTERN INTERRUPT, HOOK, STORY, ONE KEY TAKEAWAY, CTA/OFFER

all need to be encapsulated in the precise places that the skip reader will look:

- Headline/subheadings
- Figure/Figure Title
- Callouts
- First sentence
- Last paragraph.

In the example below from a whitepaper that I wrote, the Figure includes a picture of a timing report.

Most people would have just labeled this. "An example of the Timing Report"

I instead used the figure title to highlight one of the key messages of my paper.
The skip reader will receive my message because they will read figure titles.
My message is that my software allows you to generate a timing report for yourself and that you can then use the report to debug a design.

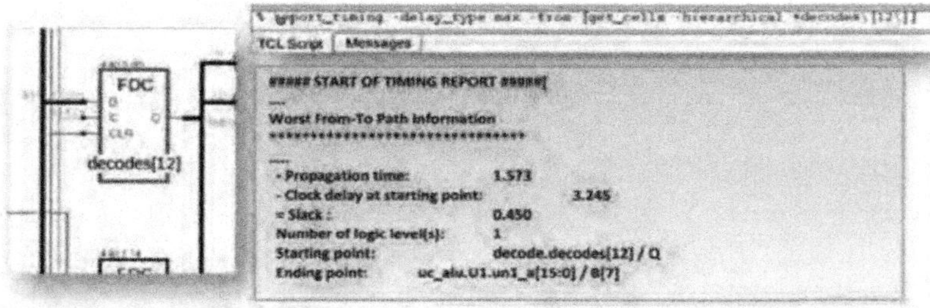

Figure 4 – You can generate timing reports to debug specific nodes in the design.

Reference: Xilinx XCELL Journal, THIRD QUARTER 2014

Where exactly should you place your Pattern Interrupt, Hook, Story, One Key Takeaway and CTA in your article or whitepaper?

The figure below provides a guideline.
For example, include your call to action in the last paragraph of your article or paper.

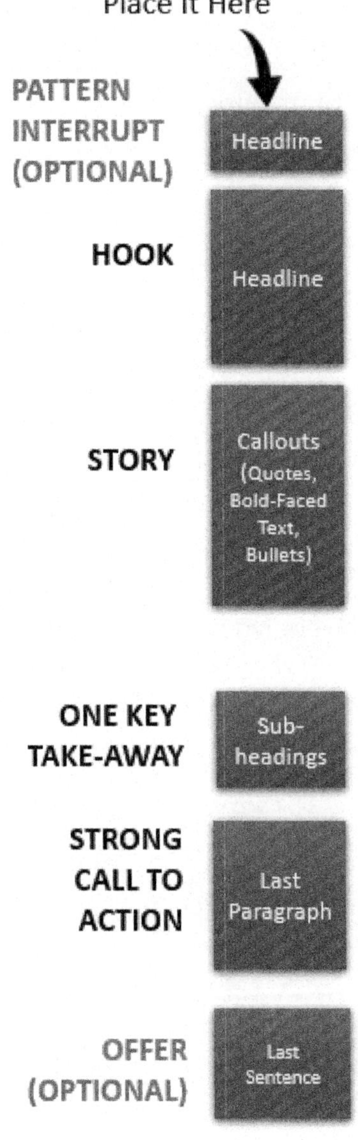

Mimic the blueprint example below to create a whitepaper/article/journal that conveys your entire message to a skip reader

Place It Here

PATTERN INTERRUPT (OPTIONAL)	 Headline	**Unusual Thing That Captures The Eye** (e.g., Picture that customer can self-identify with) Picture of stressed manager pouring over their project list. Fire coming out of the project list.
HOOK	 Headline	**Title And Intro** **What's In It For Me? What Makes Them Curious?** (e.g. A cliffhanger question. A question customers always has, makes them need to know more and pay attention Do engineering teams who use project management tools truly get the job done faster?
STORY	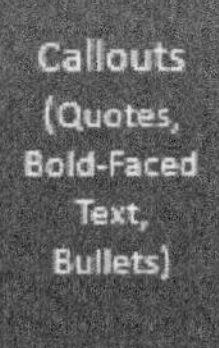 Callouts (Quotes, Bold-Faced Text, Bullets)	**Pick One:** Origin Story, Key Point Story, Case Study, Product Story, Connection Story, Overcoming Objection Story, Free PR (Point Of view/Vision/Behind the scenes/ my big mistake/2-paths) Working at a startup company... Engineering team didn't want the bureaucracy of PM tools. Then Release 8.8 tanked. Had to retract a release because it was so unstable. How I felt badly for our customers. Hurt our customer relationships... The positive outcome after applying PM software from then onward and process changes that the PM tools made apparent that we needed___
ONE KEY TAKE-AWAY	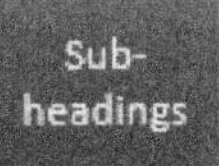 Sub-headings	**Feature – Result – Desires Met, A-Ha. I Care** Releases had less in them and were stable. We had a release process. Could see if we were behind schedule.... People not left working till midnight to get releases out
STRONG CALL TO ACTION	 Last Paragraph	**One Thing that you Want Audience to do Next** (e.g., Register for an evaluation here. Watch video. Join User Group Community) Join our 20-minute training webinar to find out how to get started using our PM tool for free
OFFER (OPTIONAL)	 Last Sentence	**PRODUCT + URGENCY + OBJECTION REMOVERS + RESULTS CREATORS** Free action sheets to give you clarity on your release approach – Which one works for you? Plus Two-weeks' free software trial and setup + migration + onboarding support

Let's take a look at three examples:

In Article/Whitepaper 1, the skip reader path is highlighted in bold.

The article contains no pictures and so we get our entire message across as follows:

- Pattern Interrupt and Hook are in the Headline
- Story (the most important part of it) appears in bold font.
  All the key elements of a story: character, mission/vision, roadblock, stakes, result/transformation are in bold font. I have labelled them in the example, for your reference.
- One Key Takeaway (feature – result – desires) is in the underlined Sub-headings
- Call To Action with an Offer can be found in the Last paragraph (in bold)

We do not use a pattern interrupt in this example.

Notice how our offer at the end contains all the required elements of an offer. Our software product plus result creators, objection removers and urgency.

Article/Whitepaper Example 1

HOOK **Do engineering teams who use project management tools truly get the job done faster?**

STORY "What? No program manager or detailed project plan for software releases?" I gasped. I had just joined a software startup team to take over business responsibility for managing their flagship product.

(Main Character) Every time **I raised the project planning and monitoring question, I became dumbfounded when I got resistance to the idea of hiring a program manager.**

I knew full well what a godsend a program manager was: the glue that kept software releases on track; made hard calls about what went into a release and what didn't; flagged risk factors early.

So why the resistance from my colleagues?

Some people in startups think that Program Management (PM) and the PM tools are for big bureaucratic companies

Many think PM tools and managers are only necessary in small companies selling to markets where quality of service is considered mission-critical: military, aerospace, medical, infrastructure and automobile applications.

I get it. Using project management tracking tools to track software project releases seems like a lot of overhead when you are in start-up momentum mode, where time is short.

(Mission / Vision) But let me ask you this.... **What is the cost to your business of a software release mistake? a poor quality release that upsets your customers? a release that is months late?**

You see, we had a talented pool of engineers that communicated well and produced amazing work.

Then along came Release 3.5 of our software; a release number forever etched in my memory.

We had grown our customer base, more customers demanding more features.
We felt immense pressure to get release 3.5 out the door and this had added complexity to the software and compressed our testing schedule.

<u>Our developers were stretched to the max</u>

Corners got cut as we checked in fragments of software code for which testing had been somewhat ad-hoc. Developer fatigue was rampant due to the high demands on their time over the past six months.

We had made some major changes to the software, per customer request and, feeling gutsy and excited about what lay ahead, thought we were in OK shape.

We were not.
The release slipped by a month… and then it slipped again by 3 weeks…

(Stakes) **The customers who wanted the new features ... and salespeople whose commissions depended upon maintaining a good customer relationship** … were up in arms. The pressure was on!
And so, after several sleepless nights working around the clock to get the release completed and tested, out it went with much fanfare... and huge sighs of relief.

Customers optimistically upgraded their software to version 3.5 but, right away, it became apparent that something was wrong.

(Roadblocks) **Customers were reporting how the new release broke their design flows, how they could no longer get their work done.**

Support tickets kept pouring in

So, we did what we had never done before.

We retracted the release.

Customers reverted to the previous stable version of the software.

Faced with still needing to deliver the new features and bug fixes that version 3.5 promised, damage control was in full force along with the need to repair our customers' trust in our development processes.

It was at that point that we made the decision to put program management in place.

We moved from an ad-hoc process ... to software schedule and quality PREDICTABILITY

We put PM tools to work, spearheaded by a newly-hired program manager who owned management of our software process.

We could now see if release deliverables were on track and where we were falling short, ensuring both stability and quality.

Using the PM tools also brought some best practices to light; tools that forced us to rethink our release process.

We realized that customers needed regular release schedules that incorporated and rolled up bug fixes.

The horrible experience with version 3.5 was a blessing in disguise, moving us to a "train release model" routine of releasing software like clock-work on a fixed schedule:

If a new feature met quality, development and test milestones then it was allowed on the current release train.

If it missed its milestones? Then the new feature had to wait for a *later* release train.

When all was said and done, one of our staff members recounted:

(Transformation and results)

"Project management tools kept us honest and forced us to prioritize.
The tools helped us to justify saying "No" or "OK" to questions about what would be in a release.
I feel less stressed by far.
I feel like we are doing a better job for our customers "

One Key Takeaway

PM tools grant you a faster time from concept to delivery, with higher product quality.

The one thing that fixed our stressful, unpredictable release process where our stated roadmap was not trusted by our customers, with release dates disbelieved and contents dicey ... was the PM software.

It tracked whether we were meeting criteria for both quality *and* development.

The PM software tracked bug fixes... It purposefully scheduled testing time and quality testing "bash" days in which our Field Application Engineers all pitched in to try the new software out before it was released.

The result? Faster time from concept to delivery... Yes!

... but, more importantly, **more predictable quality and a schedule that customers could count on.**
We also now had a **tool that let us negotiate new features with customers in a way that preserved the customer relationships and business for the long-term. Better customer retention.**

Our staff not left working till midnight to get releases out. There was less tension and call volume for our customer support staff after a release went into production.

You can do the same using the exact templates that we used, incorporated into a simple PM tool.

CTA with Offer

If you are an executive, product manager or manage development and quality assurance, join our 30-minute training webinar on Tues July 21st at 10am Pacific time

You will find out how to **try this for yourself, while getting time-limited access to our project management examples, bonus scripts and training.**
.... or feel free to *email us at (email address)*

When you call or attend the webinar, you'll receive
free action sheets that analyze the good and bad of your current release approach.

Plus **two weeks' free trial of the PM software.**
Plus "done-with-you" setup + migration + on-boarding support from our team of experts

White paper/article Examples 2 and 3 follow the "Sell Bigger" framework.

In style, they are more persuasive than Example 1.

The three elements of persuasion that they use are :

1. *Showcase a "Big idea"...* that shapes a *new belief* and kills an old one.
   How?
   They show the reader that the source of their pain and what stands in their way of getting out of pain is their old belief.
2. Show *empathy* for the reader.
3. *Remove the most common buying objections* and things standing in the way of a purchase.

Article/Whitepaper Example 2

HOOK **Should start-ups looking to get to cashflow positive either focus on one small market when seeking to engage their first 10 customers, or cast a net wide?**

STORY **Many people think that if they chase a broad market, they increase their chance of hitting the jackpot and making more sales.**

(Empathy) I get it – I've been exactly where you are, too. I didn't want to limit myself to a small market in case it didn't pan out, and **I wanted to make the case to investors that my "Total Addressable Market" was huge...**

I had convinced myself that it was good to go after a broad market.

And then this happened...

(Shape New Belief) Let me tell you a story about what happened when **I decided to first focus my start-up on a niche market.**

I asked my first customers why, in the face of more established companies, they bought from us ... and this is what they told me... that it was because we were specialists at providing exactly what they needed.

(Objection Remove) You are probably thinking that investors won't believe that your company is a good place to plant their money. The reality is that **if you start with a niche market and build success and a name there, you can next expand into adjacent markets from a position of strength**, while continuing to charge a respectable price.

One Key Takeaway **You can charge more if you specialize in a niche market**

Focusing on one market means you will appeal to this market with a specialist solution that both differentiates you from the "gorillas"... and lets you charge more. Yes – **You can charge more because you are perceived as an expert. Your solution will be perceived as a better fit: more turnkey, more focused customer support. LESS RISKY.**

It lets you establish a sustainable revenue stream that will attract investors and additional customers in that niche.
You are then financially positioned to move into adjacent markets.

CTA **Find out how you can specialize without changing your product.**

Click on this link to find out for free how you too can first succeed with a "specialist solution", for which you can charge more, and then do it again and again in adjacent markets.

The article at this link will allow you to create a solid revenue foundation for your business and deliver a highly focused solution that will make a specific segment of customers happy.

Article/Whitepaper Example 3

HOOK **Does working on two things at once make you more efficient?**

Do you multitask? And, if so, why?

(Empathy) I get it.
You have a calendar that looks like a scrabble board – full of meetings. You are sometimes double-booked.

How can you get any real work done?
You try to work on something else during a meeting ...and hope that people won't mind or notice. But then you feel like you are not getting either the meeting or your stealth task done very well..."

STORY The question of whether or not multi-task was a good idea was nagging at me in my head...

I decided to try an experiment, and this is what happened
....Let me tell you a story about how **I spent a week working on singular focused tasks instead of multi-tasking.**
I trimmed tasks from my day to accommodate it... and then observed how this made me and my customers feel

(Shape New Belief) I focused on one thing at a time.
And here is what I discovered.
People's feelings are not hurt when you tell them "No" to a task that you would have to cram into your schedule at the last minute.
When I stopped multitasking it made me realize that I had been **trading off my own priorities for other people's, whenever I accepted a new "last minute" task**...

<u>I became more disciplined in taking on additional work</u>
I got the **satisfaction of doing each task well**, to my high standard.
I was in a better position to feel good about saying "No" to certain tasks that interfered with my current plans. But here's the biggest benefit.

(Remove Objection) **<u>Working on single tasks one at a time forced me to protect my time and prioritize essential tasks.</u>**

You are probably thinking that this won't work for you – It's hard to say "No"

.... but the reality is that if you document how you spend time, you realize that you can trim a lot from it and can budget your time better –
To accommodate high value tasks first and foremost.

And **once you have that laser focus, it empowers you...**
You default to wanting to work on your project and other requests around you become background noise.
Those requests have to be well-founded before you will agree to take them on.

One Key Takeaway **<u>Doing two things at once takes more time, yields lower quality results and stresses you out.</u>**
I discovered that I delivered higher quality results with lower stress when I stopped multi-tasking.
I have more happiness and productivity tips like this in my "Power Your Day" webinar.

CTA **Click here if you want to find out how to get more done every day, with less stress.**
You will learn how to run with your own personal priorities, rather than being pulled in multiple directions by other peoples' agendas and requests.

Summary

Most whitepaper, journal and article authors unknowingly fail to accommodate the majority of readers for whom they are writing – the *skip reader*.

They also fail to clearly articulate a single compelling takeaway and then drive to the next step.

Why does this matter?
ROI.
When the whitepaper, journal or article does not convey a convincing message because it was not consumed, the customer will, of course, not be self-motivated to take the next step toward a sale.
You may gain a lead by requesting an email address in return for the whitepaper download. Yet, this lead will remain a cold and unqualified lead if they don't read the whitepaper.

For this reason, I suggest that you reformat articles, journals and whitepapers so that they do two things:

1. **Accommodate the "skip reader",** in addition to the long-form reader to ensure that all readers receive the message contained in your whitepaper, article or journal.
2. **Use the five-step "Sell Bigger" framework to get the reader's attention, keep it and drive them to the next step.** That is, use the following structure for your whitepaper, journal or article:

   Pattern Interrupt, Hook, Story, One key takeaway, Call To Action

To cater to the skip reader, insert all five steps of the "Sell Bigger" framework in the places where the reader's eyes will drift to, that is

- The Pattern Interrupt and Hook should be placed in the article/whitepaper/journal Headline.

- A Story, that is – Character, mission, roadblock, stakes, result/transformation should all be bolded in the text.
- The One Key Takeaway (feature – benefit – desires) of the article should be placed within a Sub-heading or sub-headings.
- The Call To Action and optional Offer should be placed in the last paragraph, in bold.

Chapter 13

Turn Your Website Into a Sales Machine

Create High Impact Web Pages and Online Sales Funnels

"The people who are exceptionally good in business aren't so because of what they know but because of their insatiable need to know more."

—Michael Gerber

I was conducting research that would let me teach my sales team to “sell against the competition”.

The first place I gazed in my research?

My competitors’ websites.

How did they position product benefits?

What markets were they targeting?

How were they claiming to be unique?

And how did they use their website to get leads and engage customers?

A study by Google/Millward Brown Digital showed that B2B prospects are 57% down the path to buying before they engage with you, that is before they take an action such as contacting you.

Customers do their own research and product comparisons before they contact you.

They are making a decision, not for themselves but for their company.

Yet with all that, Gerald Zaltman, a Harvard Business School professor, says that 95% of purchase decisions take place unconsciously due to the customer’s emotions.

Your website is key to putting a best foot forward in the eyes of a customer.

Yet, if you want the best chance of selling, you need to cater to the customer's emotional needs.

More.

If your website is only sending information in one direction, to the customer, for example, by offering PDF downloads or a webinar, you are missing out on a massive sales opportunity.

Why?
As I perused competitor websites, one thing became clear.

Most were very dry.

Very few felt as though they were truly engaging or fascinating to me.
Many were loaded with data that appealed to the logical side of my brain.
They were light on stories, case studies and personal experiences that could have activated the emotional side of my brain.

Very few guided me into a strong pre-sales process - a sequence of web pages that drove me further into their sales funnel – an *online sales funnel* in other words

At best, there was a whitepaper or recorded webinar registration form that attempted to get my contact information for use as a lead.

That is where the interaction ended.

Web pages – A Sales Opportunity Often Missed

On your website, you likely already have sales "lead forms" that tempt people to register for a webinar, masterclass, or to download a white paper.

This web page is the start of a potential engagement with a customer in order to prime a sale.

But here's the thing.
Many technology companies jump right into a follow up call with customers who register.

And, like the feeling you get when you walk into a shop and the sales assistant descends on you right away rather than letting you browse, a customer might walk away, scared off .... or simply ignore your offer of help.
What is even worse?.....
You might well be wasting your sales team's time with these leads that are, frankly, cold leads at this stage.

The truth? It's too early to contact most of these leads.

What can you do to optimize your chance of getting *good quality, warmed up leads* and *converting* them into a sale?

For sure, the focus of any webpage should be *conversion*.
It's the same idea as when you talk to a customer.
– You focus on what it takes to convert them,
and you lay out a set of steps that drive forward toward the sale.
In each step, you make it as easy as possible for a qualified customer to say "Yes".

But there is usually more than just one single step in face to face sales engagement. There are multiple steps in the sales process...

To make the customer connect with you further so that they "like and trust" you, and to remove their objections, for example.

Each step "micro-commits" the customer.

You can replicate this step-by-step process on your website with an online sales funnel

In this chapter, we will see some great examples.

But first let's study what people do wrong on their sales webpages ... and how to fix it.

Why Do Web Pages Fail To Convert Customers?

What are the top reasons your web pages are failing to convert a viewer into a *buyer*?

1. **No next step. No warm-up**

   Once the customer registers for a whitepaper, webinar or masterclass, the website misses out on driving a deeper online experience that pre-sells the product.
   The deeper engagement model is something that I will term an **online sales funnel.** We will discuss it further in a moment

   Using an online sales funnel, once I download a white paper or register for a webinar or master-class, the website could have:

- Driven me onward into a free challenge where we solved a single small problem together.
- Followed up my download of a white paper with a four-part email "nurturing the customer" sequence that slowly educated me and showed me how much they cared. That changed my point of view.
  A set of videos, for example that changed how I felt and thought about the "problem" that they solved,
- Qualified me, as a potential customer based on how I interacted with and consumed the follow up materials

  TIP: Your Registration's "Thank You" Page is a valuable piece of real estate that should drive the customer onward toward the sale.
  Have the registration trigger the customer's entry into an engaging online sales funnel. We will explore how to do this in the remainder of this chapter

2. **Too many choices of what to do next**

   Most web pages have links and buttons galore. This is tantamount to offering more than one obvious next step for the visitor to take.....

   When there are "choices", instead of the customer making an AUTOMATIC response (press the one and only button), the customer pauses to contemplate which option to take – and might well pick none.

   TIP: I recommend that you have only one "next step"- A single Call To Action - on your sales webpage

3. **Requires the customer to scroll down in order to take the next step**

   The Call To Action (CTA) button or link is not at the top of the page.

   Chapter 8 discusses the CTA button and link in depth.

   TIP: Your CTA button should be "above the fold". That is, the CTA button should not require the user to scroll down in order to click it.
   70% of the public will read your page on a mobile device, so your "take the next step" link or button must also be visible at the top of the page on a mobile device, no scrolling required.

4. **Too much information**

   A confused, overwhelmed buyer always says "no".

   TIP: Focus on one key takeaway message –the one thing that you want customers to remember (A Feature, Result and the Desire that it meets, for example). Refer to Chapter 7's "One Key Takeaway".

5. **No urgency**

Look at your web page, and ask, "Why should my customer act now?"

TIP: On your webpage, give your customer a reason to act:
For example, a deadline, limited-time availability of a bonus that accompanies the sale, an event on a specific date.

6. **Too many fields to fill out on the lead form section.**

Registration drops off rapidly when you have more than two fields to fill out. Yet, for your own convenience in routing the lead to the right regional sales rep, you might ask for a company name, address.....
and, in doing so, annoy the customer enough that they don't register, or simply include fake information.

Consider this: When Expedia removed one simple form field, their sales skyrocketed: That one form field cost them $12M / year

TIP: Try to limit the information you seek in your email form to "name and work email address". The priority is to get a lead so you can engage!

7. **Registration form does not anticipate that a fake email address might be submitted.**

TIP: Be really clear on your registration form that the whitepaper or webinar/masterclass details will be sent privately to the email address entered.

Create An Online Sales Funnel

I want you to think of your website sales page as the top of an online sales funnel, not as a website page per se.
Think of your website as a sales funnel –that drives customers to the next step, then the next, qualifying and showing them a single actionable next step ... each step of the way

Here is an example of an online sales funnel – four emails sent to someone after they register for a webinar/masterclass or whitepaper.

Each email drives your new lead to four educational videos, hosted on a webpage.
What does this do? It warms up the customer.

Each webpage should have a single call to action such as "click here to set up a call"

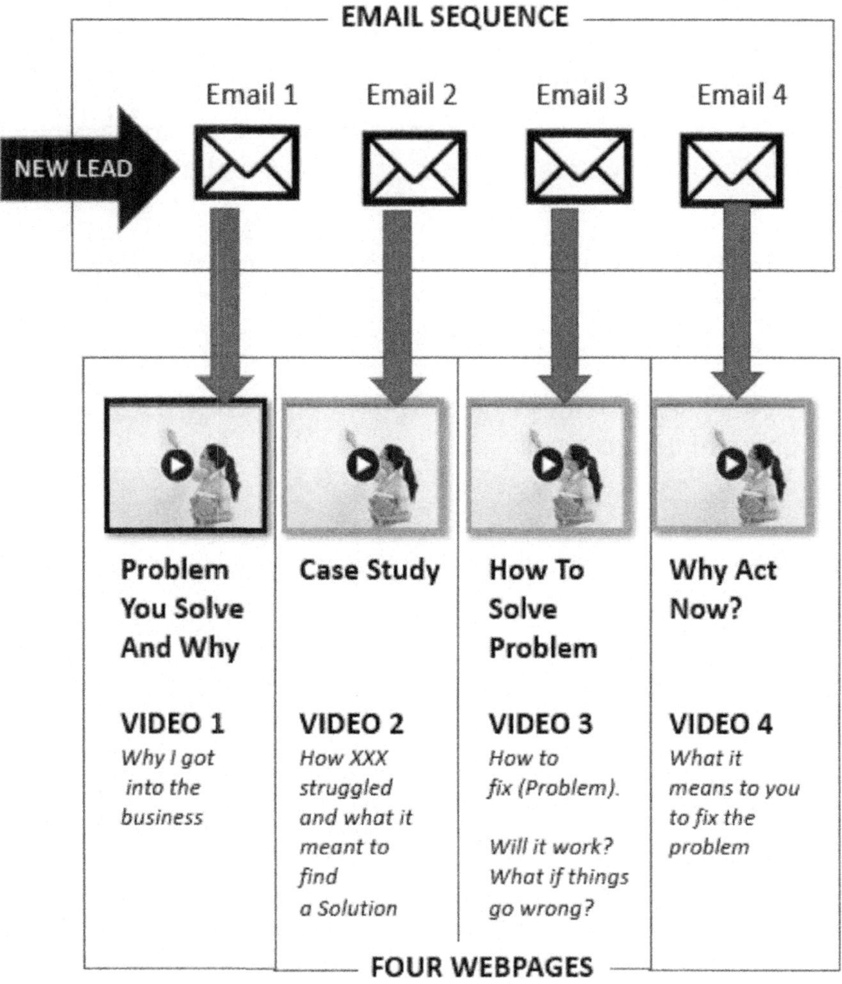
EMAIL SEQUENCE
Email 1
Email 2
Email 3
Email 4
NEW LEAD
Problem You Solve And Why
VIDEO 1
Why I got into the business
Case Study
VIDEO 2
How XXX struggled and what it meant to find a Solution
How To Solve Problem
VIDEO 3
How to fix (Problem).
Will it work? What if things go wrong?
Why Act Now?
VIDEO 4
What it means to you to fix the problem
FOUR WEBPAGES

Registration Page Examples

An online sales funnel is a massive opportunity to warm up a customer.
The result? Good and well-qualified leads...
customers that are pre-sold on what you offer before you talk on the phone.

In my "Pre-Sold" training course, I teach exactly how to build the stages of your online sales funnel.

But for now, let's just focus on the registration page that lies at the top of the funnel – It's layout is key to ensuring a high conversion rate.

I will use the Sell Bigger Framework to create the text for the landing page.

The registration page is often called a **"landing page".**

In this chapter, I will showcase landing page for:

- A free training Masterclass or Webinar
- An e-book/PDF in return for the customer's email address
- A free consultative call
- "Sign up for a FREE Software Trial"
- Join a "FREE software challenge" –
  A challenge is a way to get customers to try your software and gain one quick success.
  Hint: A challenge is a massively powerful pre-sales tool since it involves high levels of engagement. When the customer gets a result for themselves, it becomes very easy to sell to them.

Free Training, Masterclass, Webinar

HOOK + CTA HEADLINE	**<What's In It For Me>** **<Curiosity>** Get FREE Masterclass and bonuses
SUB-HEADLINE	Learn how to do/get RESULT even if you have <specific fear / obstacle / excuse>
STORY Optional Video – STORY RESULT, WHAT TO EXPECT, CTA	 < One paragraph. How we helped someone overcome OBSTACLE to get RESULT>
1 KEY TAKEAWAY	At the end of the Masterclass, you will know - How To Get RESULT - How To Overcome OBSTACLE
OFFER/CTA WHY ACT NOW?	The Masterclass is available for free until <deadline> View before <deadline> and receive <bonus training>, free T-shirt, free e-book
DO THIS NEXT	Get FREE Masterclass and bonuses

Lead Generation E-Book or PDF In Return For Email Address

HOOK + CTA

HEADLINE

SUB-HEADLINE

<What's In It For Me>

<Curiosity>

Email address

Email me my FREE E-Book

In this FREE E-Book, learn the exact step-by-step system that will do/get RESULT, even if you have <specific fear / obstacle / excuse>

STORY

Optional Video – STORY RESULT, WHAT TO EXPECT, CTA

< One paragraph. How we helped <someone> overcome OBSTACLE to get RESULT>

1 KEY TAKEAWAY

In this E-Book, discover

- The Five-step system that is getting my customers RESULT even if FEAR
- How To Overcome / How Customer Overcame OBSTACLE
- The top 3 mistakes that people make when trying to get RESULT .... and how to avoid them

OFFER/CTA

WHY ACT NOW?

DO THIS NEXT

The E-book is available for free

Sign up before <deadline> and receive early bird <bonus training>

Email address

Email me my FREE E-Book

Schedule FREE Consultative Call

HOOK + CTA

HEADLINE

SUB-HEADLINE

<What's In It For Me> Email address

<Curiosity> Schedule My Blueprint Call

Get a FREE customized Blueprint where we will together create the exact steps that you need to take to move forward and get RESULT, even if you have <specific fear / obstacle / excuse>

STORY

Optional Video – STORY RESULT, WHAT TO EXPECT, CTA

< One paragraph. Find out how we helped <someone> to overcome OBSTACLE to get RESULT>

1 KEY TAKE-AWAY

Whether or not you decide to work with us, we will develop a customized blueprint for you that

- Outlines a Step-By-Step Process To **Get From Where You Are Now To RESULT, Customized To Your Specific Needs**
- Uncovers **What's Really Standing In Your Way** So That You Can Deal With This, Head-On
- Avoids the **top 3 mistakes that people make** – Learn how to recognize that you are making them and **how to avoid them**

OFFER/CTA

WHY ACT NOW?

DO THIS NEXT

Enter your email address before DEADLINE and hit the button.
The system will then prompt you to **pick a date and time for your complementary blueprint call**

Email address | Schedule My Blueprint Call

Sign Up For Free Software Trial (SAAS)

HOOK + CTA
HEADLINE

SUB-HEADLINE

STORY
Optional Video – STORY
RESULT, WHAT TO EXPECT, CTA

1 KEY TAKEAWAY

OFFER/CTA
WHY ACT NOW?

DO THIS NEXT

<What's In It For Me> <Curiosity>

Email address

→ Get Instant Software Access Now For Just $1

Sign up, for $1 and see all that SOFTWARE has to offer for 14 days. 100% risk-free. Cancel anytime.

<One paragraph. This helped someone overcome OBSTACLE to get RESULT>

- <FEATURE1> <BENEFIT1> So That You Can ____
- <FEATURE2> <BENEFIT2> So That You Can ____
- <FEATURE3> <BENEFIT3> So That You Can ____
- Instant full access to SOFTWARE (all features)

Sign Up before DEADLINE and receive these complementary gifts:

- **<bonus training> that shows you how 5 of our customers use the software**
- **10 templates to hit the ground running**

Email address | Get Instant Software Access For $1

Sign Up For Free Software Trial (SAAS) - Example 2

HOOK + CTA

HEADLINE

SUB-HEADLINE

Fill Out The Form To Get Access To the Software and Bonuses

Sign up, for $1 and see all that <SOFTWARE> has to offer for 14 days. 100% risk-free.
Cancel anytime. Simply fill out the form

→ Get Instant Software Access Now

STORY and 1 KEY TAKEAWAY
"It works"
Testimonials/
Customer quotes

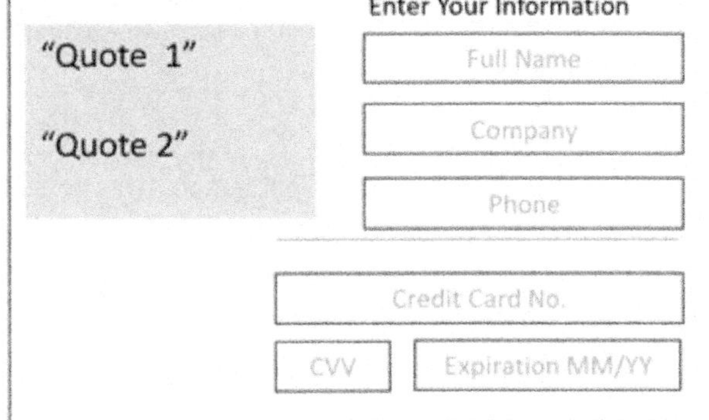

OFFER/CTA

WHY ACT NOW?

DO THIS NEXT

Sign up, and get rid of <PAIN> <LIMITED TIME OFFER>

Item	Amount
Product	$1 Then $47/mo. After 14 days

Cancel anytime, no questions asked

→ Get Instant Software Access Now

SAAS – Join The Challenge

(Get Customers Hooked On Your Software Via A Quick Success)

HOOK + CTA HEADLINE	**<What's In It For Me> <Curiosity>** [Email address] → Join The Challenge For Just $1
SUB-HEADLINE	Sign up for the Three-day Challenge
STORY Optional Video – STORY RESULT, WHAT TO EXPECT, CTA	[Video] The Challenge helped <someone> overcome OBSTACLE to get RESULT. **Here's what you get:**
1 KEY TAKEAWAY	• **<u>Day 1</u>: Implement <BENEFIT1> So That You Can ____** • **<u>Day 2</u>: Learn how to <BENEFIT2> So That You Can ____** • **<u>Day 3</u>: See <RESULT> So That You Can ____** • **Instant full access to SOFTWARE (all features) for 14 days** • **Templates, Step-By-Step Instructions, Live Daily Q&A conducted via An Exclusive Facebook Community**
OFFER/CTA WHY ACT NOW? DO THIS NEXT	The **Challenge starts on <deadline>** **Sign Up before DEADLINE and receive <bonus pre-training>, templates, <other>** [Email address] Join The Challenge For $1

SAAS – Join The Challenge – Example 2

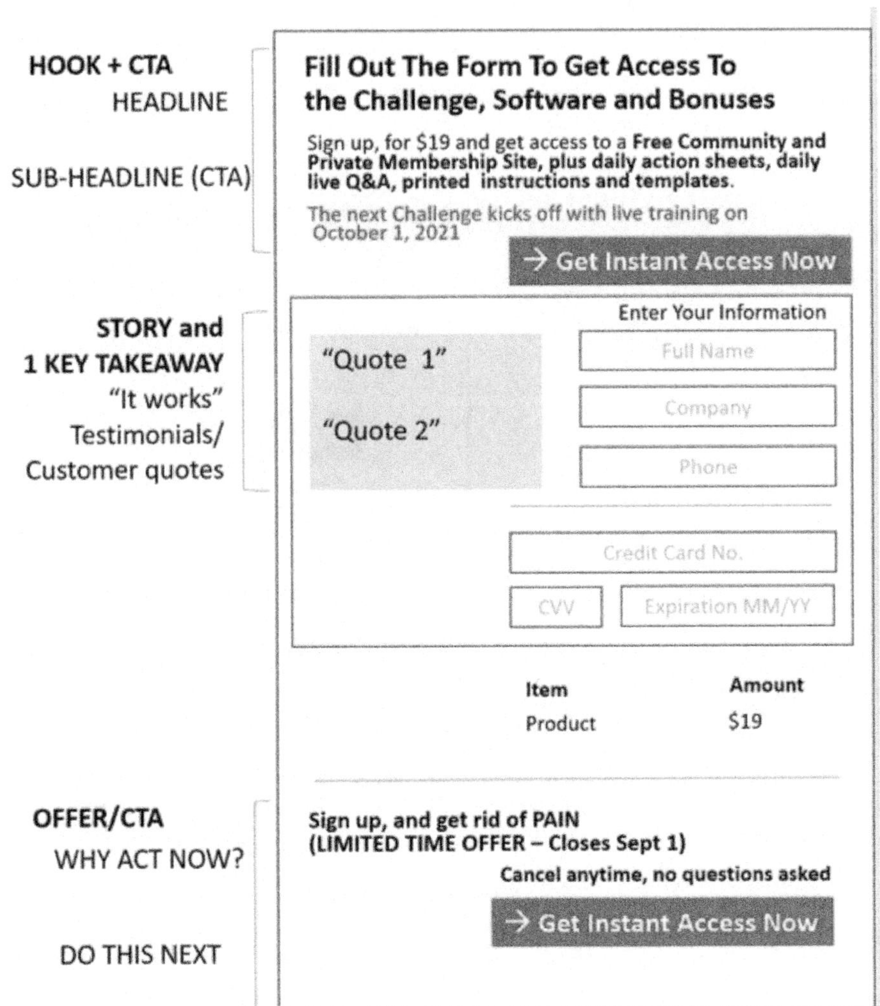
HOOK + CTA
HEADLINE
SUB-HEADLINE (CTA)
Fill Out The Form To Get Access To the Challenge, Software and Bonuses
Sign up, for $19 and get access to a Free Community and Private Membership Site, plus daily action sheets, daily live Q&A, printed instructions and templates.
The next Challenge kicks off with live training on October 1, 2021
→ Get Instant Access Now
STORY and
1 KEY TAKEAWAY
"It works"
Testimonials/
Customer quotes
"Quote 1"
"Quote 2"
Enter Your Information
Full Name
Company
Phone
Credit Card No.
CVV
Expiration MM/YY
Item
Amount
Product
$19
OFFER/CTA
WHY ACT NOW?
DO THIS NEXT
Sign up, and get rid of PAIN
(LIMITED TIME OFFER – Closes Sept 1)
Cancel anytime, no questions asked
→ Get Instant Access Now

Summary

When a customer performs product research on your website with a view to a possible purchase, how can you turn that interested viewer into a qualified customer that buys?

What you need is the equivalent of a sales funnel… online. Online pages and email sequences that drive a customer down a specific path with the goal of *conversion*.

Funnels are covered in much more detail in my online "PRE-SOLD" training course.

If your website pages that deliver free webinars and white paper downloads lack a next step of engagement on the "thank you" page, you are missing an opportunity to drive customers further down into an online sales funnel.

That is, you are throwing away the opportunity to have existing customers buy more or new prospects buy for the first time.

How should you reformat your website sales pages to maximize the chance that you get good leads and determine existing customer interest in buying more from you?

You can do this by reformatting you web registration forms into landing pages as shown in the examples in this chapter. These landing pages do the following in order to maximize conversion:

- Make it easy for the customer to register (few fields to fill out).
- A heading that includes curiosity and WIIFM
- Story and one key takeaway that convinces the customer that your solution works – a case study, for example.
- A reason to act now

- What to do next - include a *single* CTA… that makes the next step you want the customer to take easy to take, a bright button, "above the fold", for example.

Once the customer registers at the landing page, a follow up sequence is triggered

- A sequence of nurturing emails and/or
- A sequence of web pages that the customer then experiences.
  Something that drives the customer step-by-step closer to the sale.

It's my hope that the examples in this chapter help you.
They show you how to get leads via a free PDF download, a Webinar or Masterclass.
The examples also show how to get sign-ups for a free software trial or five-day challenges, or a consultative call.
These example landing pages are the first step toward getting qualified customers to enter your sales funnel

Use them as a model for your own website sales pages.

Chapter 14

High Impact Video

Bring Customers Closer

"Life is meant to be shared"

—Josh Groban from the song: "Your Face"

In the mid 20th Century, one of the few ways you could see a video or movie was from the seat of a car.

In fact, the first drive-in movie theater, a cinema consisting of a large outdoor movie screen with the viewers' cars parked in front of it, was created in Las Cruces, New Mexico, USA on April 23rd, 1915.

By the 1940's, hundreds were opening each year. The concept is romanticized in movies such as *Grease*.

In that era, the video cameras used to capture the movies were immense and cumbersome machines and recordings made using large reels of film.

Fast forward to today: we have Cable, Satellite and Streaming services such as Netflix. This is all that we consumers need for a great movie experience in the comfort of our own home.

And if you have a smartphone, you have almost everything you need to create your very own mini-movie – A video.

So where should you start?

How can you create a video that someone will actually watch and remember?

The principles behind creating a video are, in fact, similar to those used to create an email.

Except that we need to take the plunge and get in front of the camera!

In this chapter, we will use the "Sell Bigger Framework" to create our video.

That is

Pattern-Interrupt - Hook – Story – One Key Takeaway – Call To Action

But before you start to get nervous about the idea of making a video for your customer, let's make you feel a whole lot more confident about the concept.

Let's explore some of the myths that get in the way of creating sales videos, how to reframe them in your mind, and what to do to become great on camera.

Video-Making Myths That Scare You, And How To Overcome The Fear

Why do so many people never get around to making videos? Why do some actually live in fear or avoid creating videos for their new and existing customers?

There are several things that people tell themselves that get in their way. They are:

Myth 1 – My video needs to be perfectly produced.

Truth – Videos in which you look like a regular person (a.k.a. the authentic you) usually convert better than fancy or pretty videos.

Myth 2 – I need fancy video equipment.

Truth – Use your smartphone. If filming a distance away from the phone, use a wireless microphone … (Audio quality is far more important than video quality).

A smartphone + optional wireless microphone is all you need.

Myth 3 – I am afraid of the camera.

Truth – This problem afflicts most people.

The root cause?
They are afraid of being judged.
How exactly can you become confident on camera?

It truly comes down to practice and building muscle/memory.

Here's what works:

Create one "practice video" per day for 10 days and you will feel confident by the end of it, getting most videos recorded on the very first take well before day 10.

Before you film.... jump up and down a couple of times to gain energy... and smile...Only then hit "RECORD"

Myth 4 – I don't have time.

Truth – After you build muscle memory, you will become confident on video.

It becomes easier to the point that it will be quicker to make a video than to type an email.
Your video is more likely to be consumed than your email's written content because it will be viewed as a more personalized communication

Which brings me to my main point...

Why make videos?

Simple.

Video increases consumption.

CUSTOMERS ARE WILLING TO WATCH A FIVE-MINUTE VIDEO but some will not be willing to read an email that takes five minutes to read, even when the video and email follow the very same script.

For some demos of your software, only a video can sufficiently demonstrate the nuances.

Using Video To Promote Sales and Renewals

When should you use video?

Here are some places to use videos:

- **Webinars or Masterclasses**
- **Product demos** to which you link, from an email sales page promotional video – Simply record the screen and then send the customer a link to your recorded video. Record the screen using *ScreenCastify, Loom, Camtasia, Zoom, Screenflow*, or *OBS*
- **Case studies** in which you interview a customer informally e.g., via a Zoom call, recorded with the customer's permission!
- **Educational videos** – Such as tips on "How to" do something
- **Connection videos to make people trust you** – A personal story with a moral, or a rant with a moral, or a story about an experience you have in common with the customer.
- **Highly personal messages** – Messages where a personal video would make you stand out and appear to care more than the average salesperson, "I recorded this video for you..."
- **To remove an objection and create a new belief so that you can persuades people to buy,** in the face of an excuse or procrastination

How To Be Visually Interesting

Your video script will keep your audience interested…

But what else might you do to enhance that, visually?

There are four languages of human communications and some examples of each:

1. **Energy** (think of Robin Williams)
2. **Visual auditory** (Authority such as Bill Gates; Stories such as Ronald Reagan)
3. **Kinesthetic** (The rich and deep voice of Barry White)
4. **Connection** (The warm and friendly voice of Morgan Freeman)

Apply all of these. How?

- Move around as you record.
- Slow down your sentence when you want to make an important point.
- Smile
- Speak with sincerity and purpose
- Make eye contact with the camera
- Make your voice friendly and flowing.

Your Video Recording Routine

Here is the routine to follow to record videos that both feel and look good.

Before getting on camera (in order):

1. Put post-it note fragment next to cellphone camera (so you remember exactly where to make eye contact)
2. Jump up and down or do a couple of jumping jacks
3. Make yourself laugh … and then smile
4. Sing a line or two to the virtual audience that you are about to help!
5. Hum for 15 seconds to warm up the vocal cords !

Hit "record" and do this:

- Use a deliberate, happy voice !
- Smile as you look at the camera
- Be animated in a way that show feelings and the passion for what you do
- Be genuine
- Use stories to garner interest !
  Use conversations (what people verbalized) within the story to keep people engaged
- Lower the tone of and slow down your voice when making a key point that you want the audience to remember

Expect to mess up and suck for the first couple of attempts.

It may take 20 iterations to get your first video done, 10 the next time you do it, then gradually decreasing each time you make a video.

The thing to remember?

Recording a video takes just three things: practice, courage and commitment.

It's well worth it - Your customers will like you even more after they see you on video.

High Impact Video – An Example Script

HOOK **This advice from Geoffrey Moore will change how you think about sales growth stories.**

STORY It was my first real job after postgraduate school – I was a software engineer, working for a computer-aided design company.

We had launched a new product and were taking on more customers.

I was pumped. We'd received a great response from early customers, thus far.

But what worked when we sold to our initial technology-enthusiastic customers didn't quite cut it for some of the new people whom we were trying to impress.
Does this sound familiar?

Geoffrey Moore describes this phenomenon as the "CHASM" in his book, *Crossing the Chasm*.

The chasm is something that technology startups and new product teams hit, right after they succeed with their first customers.

Our start-up's early customers (what Geoff calls the INNOVATOR and EARLY ADOPTER customers) had happily figured out how to use our new product, even though it was a bit rough at the edges and didn't have the best of documentation.

Since our first customers overwhelmingly succeeded, we thought that we were on a roll... We were hot stuff....

And our early customers thought that our leading-edge software was amazing.

However, we were unwittingly heading straight for the CHASM and about to fall in...

You see, to really grow the business, we were going to need to attract what Geoff calls "mainstream customers".

A mainstream customer needs more than having your cool software dumped in their lap.

--- They need what Geoffrey calls the "WHOLE PRODUCT".

That is... a complete experience that gets them from their point of pain to a point of results, *intuitively and easily.*

I am talking about things such as *help videos, onboarding, decent documentation, and local customer support personnel.*

The day I read *CROSSING THE CHASM* was the day I knew what to do to grow my software business.

I had to eat my early pride and do three things exactly as Geoffrey directed.

Firstly: Focus on a single customer niche and do whatever it takes to make them succeed.

Secondly: Deliver the complete product experience – that thing that Geoff calls "the whole product".

> What else, outside the software, did customers need..... to believe that they could get the outcome they wanted?
>
> Let's start with documentation... "How to" training, examples, templates, and ways for them to validate that what they had

accomplished with my software was "correct" so that they trusted the software.

The MAJORITY of my market also wanted quick success ....without the pain of migrating from their current solution into our new software.
So, I needed an onboarding process, integrations with the other tools that they used, and scripts that imported their designs into my software - import tools

Thirdly, I needed to be perceived as a market leader in a niche by positioning us as the *experts* in our niche...

I needed to be clear about a SINGLE BIG COMPELLING PROBLEM that we alone solved in the specific niche that we targeted

Fast forward to today and the *Crossing the Chasm* book is still my guiding light for the way that I now market on the internet.

Listen Up!

These days, it's cheaper than ever to use online marketing and training,.... specifically, using what's called an "online sales funnel" to cross the "chasm" – educate and onboard customers. Get more customers!

... AND, it's super easy to target a niche of customers with your funnel.

So, what's an online sales funnel?

One Key Takeaway

An online sales funnel is like having a group of great salespeople working for you 24/7 and walking people through the sales or a training process, except you do most of it online.

Your funnel is going to educate customers and help them solve the biggest problem in your niche… without having to ask for anything in return.

Use an online sales funnel to **automate sending sequences of bite-sized free advice and training** to people that register at your website.

How do you close the sale with the people in your online funnel? You create a compelling event with a time limited offer to create some urgency to the sale.

You can later use a funnel to train customers and onboard them to incentivize them to finish the training.
The funnel simply walks the customer through a series of training steps to follow.

CTA **If you'd like to learn more about creating an online funnel and feel like you have a whole team of salespeople working for you – nurturing and qualifying customers, click here to watch this 30-minute masterclass and enter to win ____.**

Summary

Until the 1980's, videos were largely reserved for TV, pop songs and the movies.

Today, we are fortunate: Making a video is as easy as picking up a cellphone and having a script in your head that lets you deliver a strong sales message your customers will love to watch.

Be sure that the videos you create are short, generally five minutes long or less. If the information takes longer than five minutes to convey, create a series of videos chunked into five-minute chapters.

Use the Sell Bigger Framework to structure your video's content.

That way you will get attention, keep it, get one clear message across, then drive the customer to the next step in the sale.

Create more than just "how to" videos that demo how to solve a focused problem.

Create videos to connect with customers, plus videos that shape new beliefs, convey a "big idea", and remove a sales objection.

One thing you will find that surprises you if you initially feel awkward in front of the camera – It doesn't matter. It's just part of your journey.
In the space of a few days, you will see a huge improvement in your confidence.

Make yourself create one video each day for 10 days and it will become a breeze.
It just takes practice and imagination that you are talking to a friend.

Recording a video takes practice, courage and commitment. Yet it becomes second nature within weeks of your first attempt.

Have energy, smile and your customers will love your videos and like you as a person because of them.

By making videos frequently and confidently, you will be stepping to the microphone to do the one thing that 90% of other sales professionals won't dare to do.

Chapter 15

Get Customers To Call You Back

High Impact Voicemails

Success is nothing more than a few simple disciplines, practiced every day."

—Jim Rohn

It used to really bother me when my existing customers failed to call me back, after I had left them a voicemail.

Perhaps you have the same issue?

How are you supposed to read the fact that a customer seems to be ignoring you?

Is it that your "radio-silent" customer ...

- Is not interested in talking?
- Thinks you are a pest?
- Fears that you will try to sell them something?
- Thinks that they don't have the time right now.
- Feels that your product is working well... so they don't have any urgent reason to talk.
- Is about to jump ship?
- Prefers to communicate via email rather than phone?
- Is the wrong person to talk to now, and you just don't know it?

The dilemma?

There can be many reasons why your customer doesn't return your voicemail.

If you have not reached out to this particular customer recently, it's impossible to figure out the true explanation, let alone, know what to do about it.

Meanwhile, you feel like you are being left in the lurch.

You worry that this customer might jump ship.

You are left unable to sell them more because you can't tell what they need until you have a live conversation...

The same is true for brand new sales leads who, at first encounter, seem like a perfect fit… and then they go silent on you.

"I have a hot lead….

… BUT…. I keep hitting voicemail jail when I call … What can I do?"

My inside sales team would report to me.
They were always meticulous at following up on sales leads.

We had "niched down" our product messaging to deliver information focused on military and aerospace accounts. We had created webinars and whitepapers focused on their very specific needs - tools that helped customers to create highly reliable semiconductor chips used in military and outer space applications.

We had received some extraordinary, well-qualified leads from companies that we had already sold to that we could potentially upsell … and great leads for new customers.

My webinars and whitepapers?

I'd keep them focused on one small topic and take-away… a flavor ….

That way, **customers would not be overwhelmed, and, more importantly, they were left hungry for more.**

The first step in the sales follow-up process after a webinar or whitepaper download is to send attendees the slides for the presentation or an executive summary of the content of the whitepaper with the promise that someone technical (inside sales team) will be giving them a quick call to brainstorm how we could help them.

The lead had some interest since they had downloaded the whitepaper or showed up for the webinar.

So why was it that 30% of webinar attendees never returned our follow-up call?

We tweaked our approach in order to figure out why and discovered something that was also useful for *any* kind of lead or voicemail follow-up – An approach that made the customer motivated and not too scared to return the call.

The plan?

- A voicemail under 45 seconds in length.
- The voicemail script? It consisted of five parts ... The five parts of the Sell Bigger Framework.

**Pattern Interrupt – Hook – Story –
One Key Takeaway – CTA**

Here's a voicemail example that follows the five-part Sell Bigger Framework.

Its goal is to get a customer who attended a webinar to call back.

The tone and words are genuine and customer-oriented; as if you are looking out for the customer.

The offer of help is attractive – 5 minute read of what real customers do to gain a particular success.

It implies that they need to know more than was presented in the webinar.

It asks for nothing in return.

It's very short.

The 45 Second Voicemail That Gets Customers To Call You Back

Pattern Interrupt	Hi (NAME) – I was so glad to meet you at the (WEBINAR) on (DATE) This is ___ from ___ . You can reach me at _____ .
HOOK	I have to confess that, while the webinar made things sound pretty straightforward, putting it into practice can be a lot quicker with one more piece of information.
STORY	Every time I give my customers additional examples donated by live customers ... with step-by-step instructions of what to do .... it gives them more clarity. I would like to send these examples to you.
One Key Takeaway	The examples are a five-minute read ... They include how one of our key customers solved (PROBLEM) using our software's ___ feature, so that they no longer had to worry about manually doing ____.
CTA	Give me a callback if you'd like me to send it. Once again, call me at ______ to let me know if it's OK to send it.

"Call Me Back" Voicemail Checklist

As you create a voicemail script, simply follow the checklist to motivate your customers to return your call.

1. **Relate the call to a referral to call them… or to anything your company has done for them recently.**

   "My Field Application Engineer ___ suggested that I call to help you___."

   "You attended the ___ webinar and we wondered if you would like a copy of the slides."

2. **"Do they even remember who I am?"**

   Be sure to mention your company, where you met or chatted.

   "We met at __ and were talking about ___."

3. **Have energy in your voice tone.**

   Do some jumping jacks before you call … and smile !!

4. **Use friendly and conversational words – You are watching out for them.**

   "Hey – I was thinking about you and the problem that you mentioned that you had… I think I have a way to solve it."

5. **Short and sweet (45 seconds or less)**

6. **Give a reason to call you back - WIIFM or curiosity.**

   "This <thing I am offering to send you> just helped one of my other customers do ___ and I was thinking that it would help you, too. Give me a callback and I can get you the info you need."

"I'd like to give you (GIFT/E-book) that will help you get ___.
... Leave me a message to tell me where to email it."

Summary

When existing customers or seemingly interested prospects failed to call me back, that meant one thing – I was left in the dark.

I worried that I might lose them as a customer.

I knew that it is 6-7x easier to sell to an existing customer than it is to acquire a new customer.
I was concerned I was missing out on easy sales opportunities in my existing customer accounts.

Most of all, I wanted to maintain a great relationship with my customers and serve them well.

Why was I worried?

When my customers didn't call me back, was it because they are not really interested? Thinking about jumping ship? Just too busy right now?

I found a better way to structure my voicemails; a way that gave customers the motivation and inclination to call me back.

It started by considering "what's in it for the customer" and then combining that with creating curiosity – the headline or the first thing that I said in the voicemail that I left.

Before I picked up a phone to call, you'd find me bouncing around like a bunny, a ritual that I used to build energy into my voice. It felt good.

I then crammed my voice message into 45 seconds, to maximize the chance people would listen to it in its entirety and call me back.

I followed the Sell Bigger Framework.

Pattern Interrupt - Hook – a (two-sentence or so) story – one key takeaway - a call to action to call me back.

Customers that were truly interested and perhaps just busy then *did* call me back.

“At risk” customers who felt that we didn’t care and whose renewals might lie in the balance were happy that we called. Many returned my call so that a new conversation could begin.

Model the example in this chapter and you too will see an eager response from your customers whenever you leave them a voicemail.

CONCLUSION

This book teaches a simple five-piece Framework for customer communications.

SELL BIGGER FRAMEWORK

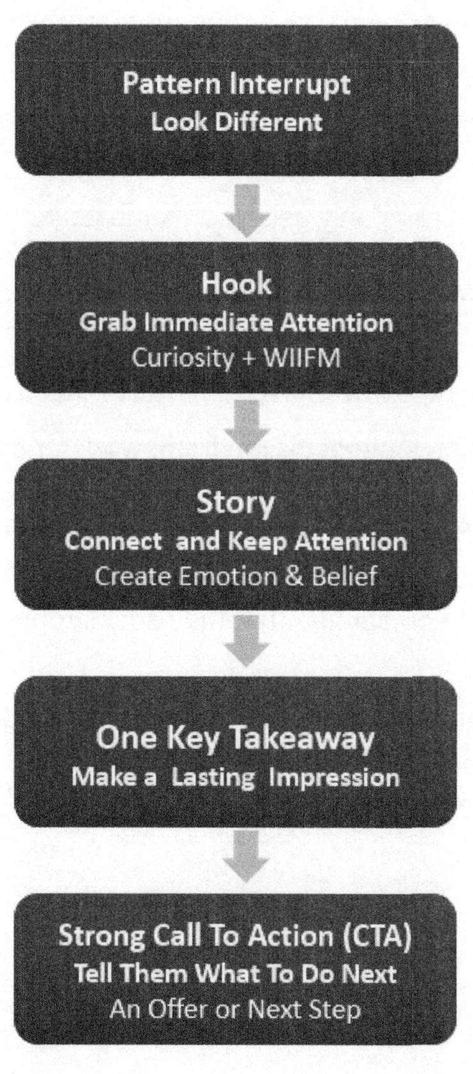

The Framework's superpower is that it makes what you communicate stand out from the crowd.
Your communication will immediately grab your customer or prospect's attention when other communications do not.

The Framework structures message headlines, titles and pattern interrupts that "jump out".

It uses stories to tap into the customer's emotions so that they listen and remember you.

It makes the message to your customer clear and punchy with just one carefully crafted key takeaway.

It then motivates your customer to take your desired next step ... using a single call to action or an offer, if they so-wish.

Because any book is only as good as the action that it inspires, the book contains examples and action sheets that will let you put the framework to work...right now.

Free electronic copies of these templates can be downloaded *https://www.marketfastfoward.com/freestuff*

It's my hope that you master the framework for success in your own emails, voicemails, webinars, masterclasses, presentations, whitepapers, videos, and online sales webpages.

And that, most of all, you have another means to show your customers that you care so that they stick around for the long-term.

My wish is that, when you use this framework, communication channels open up that let you identify new upsell opportunities in your existing accounts to further enrich your customers.

Bonus Resources

Attention, book readers!

Register to download free bonus materials here:

www.marketfastforward.com/freestuff

Bonus Materials include:

- Printable PDF copies of the Action Sheets found in this book
- Links to challenges and courses that accelerate your ability to put the Sell Bigger framework into action in your business
- Text copies of the examples in the book, so that you can use them as a basis for your own communications

Acknowledgements

To my mother, Connie Charlesworth, who is forever my inspiration in the good life that she lives and in her ethic of constant learning and curiosity. Her love springs eternal.

To Rnold Smith for solidifying in my mind "What makes people take action". https://theconnectionapp.com/

To visionary, Russell Brunson, for introducing me to the concept of "Hook, Story, Offer". I adapted this fine concept for use in software sales communication. Your energy inspires me. https://expertsecrets.com/

To my amazing editor, David Seaman, whose infinite patience, humor and attention to detail made this book possible .. and legible.

To my publisher Best Seller Publishing. To Bob Harpole for his amazing coaching throughout the creation of the book. To Rob Kosberg who continues to enlighten me every week with weekly training sessions. Working with you has been a pleasure. Your staff offloaded me and guided me with such gentle experience,

To Mike "Mac" McFarlane. In my first job out of postgrad school, you took me under your wing. You grounded me. I learnt so many life planning and communication skills from you that I continue use to this day.

To Brandon Lucero. Your coaching in the art of "thought reversal" is applied within this book to remove sales objections and is a lovely way to change a customer's way of thinking. You are an amazingly giving person and talented communicator. www.video4xeffect.com

To my belated father, Charles Charlesworth, who instilled in me the importance of helping others. With his actions, he showed just how deeply he cared for his community and country. His intelligence and humor turned science and learning into the fun that it now continues to be for me.

To the incredibly talented Dave Newton, for his assistance in branding and for helping me brainstorm book names.

To a very special entrepreneurial friend who kept me laughing like crazy and motivated throughout the authoring process. You know who you are. I don't know what I would do without you.

To my friends and former colleagues – Rich Goldman, Helena Winkler, Will Cummings, Bob Schetlick, Farzad Zarrinfar whose input led to this book. Your commitments to sales and marketing, sprinkled with fun inspire me each day.

Printed in Great Britain
by Amazon